# Great Lakes Stories

ASHORE AFTER 50 YEARS

Capt. Ray J. McGrath

# *Great Lakes Stories*

## ASHORE AFTER 50 YEARS

by
Captain Ray I. McGrath

*with illustrations by
the Captain himself*

*Border Enterprises*
Sault Sainte Marie, Michigan

Published by Border Enterprises
302 Armory Place, Sault Sainte Marie, MI 49783-2006

Cover Design by Marian B. MacLeod
Line Art by Ray I. McGrath
Printed and bound in the U.S.A.

Library of Congress Catalog Number: 96-85704


ISBN 0-9652747-0-5


The text of this book is set in New Caledonia.

Printed in the United States of America
2  3  4  5  6  7  8  9  10

This book is printed on recycled, acid-free paper.

# Dedication

My sailing career was not always smooth. I am grateful to all those who helped me along the way.

I especially wish to dedicate this book to my wife, Lou, and to my mother, who were always there when I needed them; and to my editor/publisher, Marian MacLeod of Sault Ste. Marie and Brimley, Michigan. Without her encouragement and help, this book would never have been written.

I became attached to every boat I worked on and really felt that we (the boat and I) were working together. I can understand why some captains choose to stay with their foundering vessels.

*Steady as she goes—*

*Capt. Ray J. McGrath*

# Contents

## I. Shipping Disasters

## II. Personal Shipping Stories

## III. General Shipping Stories

## IV. Personal Stories

## V. Glossary and Index

# Illustrations

# Illustrations, continued

# Preface

## Captain Ray I. McGrath of the Port of St. Ignace

Events in the annals of Great Lakes history hold a deep, mystic sway over those of us who have lived amid the waters of Superior, Michigan, Huron, Erie and Ontario. From the days when Fr. Jacques Marquette ministered to the Indians by way of canoe, until the icy water's destruction of the Edmund Fitzgerald—indeed, even to this very day—we are intrigued by stories of Great Lakes vessels and of those men who walked their decks. The lives of sailors have not been easy; many have been lost in the great storms that have made the sturdiest of vessels seem fragile in their grips. Perhaps it is the lonely, difficult, dangerous lives these sailors experienced that lead us to want to be a part of the bonding which they hold for one another.

Captain Ray I. McGrath, a good and trusted friend, has spent 50 years sailing these lakes, 24 of them as captain of a number of the Great Lakes sailing vessels. He tells a good story of sailors' lives, and the histories of many, many boats. The humor and in-depth information he provides give us a rare insight, and somehow put us into that window of time of days past, as if you and I had been there.

We are fortunate that Capt. McGrath has given the many years required to collect material and to write this book. You may remember some of the vessels from the numerous drawings he has made. Thank you, Capt. McGrath, for the hours of enjoyable reading.

*Al Dalimonte*
Mackinac County Prosecutor's Office

# Introduction

*I* began putting the stories of my Great Lakes adventures, and the history of boats on the lakes, down on paper many years ago. People who saw them or heard me tell of them encouraged me to get the stories into print.

There have been many books written about the Great Lakes, and several of them are found on the shelves of bookstores and specialty stores. The reason I have written yet another book on the subject is to give you a different perspective on lake navigation. I have had different stories and more diverse adventures from most folks because I sailed these unpredictable waters for fifty years—from 1935 to 1985.

When I sailed the lakes, things were very different from the way they are now. For instance, the largest boat in the Great Lakes when I retired was 600 feet long. Different materials are now being used to construct the ships, and different technologies are being used to run the ships. I wanted you to know how life aboard the ships was before we had radar and radio telephones. I can remember when captains had to use their stopwatches when navigating in dense fog, in order to ascertain where they were and when to turn—and hoping they were right.

Personnel matters were much different in those days, also. I never took vacations, and the only times I left the ships were twice, for family funerals—for my wife's mother and for my own father. I always enjoyed excellent health and was never involved in an accident that would prevent my working. It was hard, because I had a wife and two sons in St. Ignace. However, they would sometimes go on the ships with me. There were no unemployment checks back in those days, so I often worked as shipkeeper during the winter layup season. As you will read in the pages to follow, my wife spent quite a bit of time with me aboard the boats when she could.

Fifty years on the boats have given me many stories to share. I hope you enjoy them all as much as I have enjoyed writing about them. —*Ray J. McGrath*

# I

# Shipping Disasters

*Keep her between the buoys—*

# Lake Storms

S hips have been lost on the Great Lakes almost every year, and from nearly every cause.

There was the Big Blow of 1913, in which 19 vessels were stranded; six were driven ashore as total losses, 13 vanished completely—between 275 and 300 persons died in that storm. On Lake Huron near Goderich, Ontario, 25 frozen bodies drifted ashore, and 22 others came ashore near Thedford, Ontario.

In that same storm, a captain related how the storm struck his 500-foot freighter, the Howard M. Hanna Jr. The seas were so huge, he had no way to control his boat. The enormous waves tore off his after-cabin and the top of his pilot house, broke down the doors and windows, and poured water into the engine room.

The storm finally blew her broadside onto a reef about 10 p.m. The smokestack was gone and the lifeboats and raft carried away. At #7 hatch, a wide crack appeared across the deck and down the ship's side.

With time and better-built, more modern freighters, one would think those mishaps to be a thing of the past; however, in spite of many weather reports, modern radios and navigation equipment, we're still losing ships. For instance, in 1975, the Edmund Fitzgerald was lost without even a radio message. Twenty-nine seamen went down with her.

In 1905, in a Lake Superior storm, there were 19 vessels lost and 80 seamen dead.

The 1926 ice blockade on the Great Lakes saw 150 ships frozen in place below the Locks at the Sault. The Chief Wawatam and five tugs worked for three weeks to release all the boats but 26. These had to remain in the St. Mary's River at the Sault until spring.

I remember the grain vessel Wolverine anchored in St. Ignace harbor to ride out a northwesterly storm which lasted about a week. When the weather cleared and she was ready to go, she found herself to be frozen solid, and had to spend the winter in St. Ignace.

My last trip before retiring, I had a storage load of grain for Buffalo. We had a strong northwesterly wind as we approached Buffalo, with strong storm warnings. We were scheduled to fuel up in the outer harbor before going up the river to our winter berth. Just as we finished fueling, the wind really began to howl, but I figured I could make the elevator dock. I had to use the anchor three times before arriving at the dock. Current and wind were really strong.

I was pleased that I had my favorite old-time wheelsman with me. We made the dock safely without a tug, and didn't attempt to use the engine for a "back-up" or "reverse." The next day the chief informed me that we had a broken tail shaft, and so we wouldn't have had the use of the engine at all if we had attempted to back up. The engine had a jagged break, and meshed together so long as we were going forward. If we had put her in reverse, it would have disengaged and he'd have had nothing.

I whispered a "thank-you" to that Guy in the Sky.

Chief Wawatam

# The Hudson

*he steel package freighter Hudson was launched in* 1888 for Western Transit Co. of Buffalo, NY. She was sturdily built, exceeding the average construction cost, and valued at $250,000.

She served the company well all her life and survived many storms. However, the storm that struck the lakes on September 15, 1901, was of hurricane force, and struck the eastern half of Lake Superior. The Hudson was bound from Duluth to Buffalo with a cargo of wheat and flax when the storm hit. The storm raged on for three days, and on September 19 wreckage from a steamer was sighted. In the following days, bodies came ashore in the vicinity of Keweenaw Point. The Hudson had apparently foundered with all 24 hands somewhere off Eagle Harbor light.

Reports filtered into the newspapers about the foundering of the big steel freighter and the worst was confirmed—she was last seen by another ship which was in dire straits herself and could offer no assistance. The pilot house was found a few days later many miles away. To this day, the hull has never been found, and the direct cause of the sinking remains a mystery.

The Hudson tale is one that records the fury of fall lake storms. In my experience, I have found that the November storms usually outranked the December storms.

A few times in storms, I'd check down a little so she'd ride better. And if I could steer right into the storm I'd go to bed and get up eight hours later, only to find myself within a mile of where I'd been the night before—riding comfortably. However, occasionally I would get caught in an unpredictable storm and really begin rolling. I would stand in that front window for 12, 15, even 20 hours without leaving. Those occasions were rare.

Following are stories of some of the shipping disasters I have learned about in my years of sailing.

Stmr. Hudson
288' x 41' x 22.7

6

# The Myron

The steamer *Myron* was 186 feet in length, 28 feet wide and 12½ feet deep, a 676-ton wooden steamer originally launched in 1888 as the Mark Hopkins.

On November 22, 1919, with 700,000 board feet of lumber, towing the schooner barge Miztec carrying 1,050,000 board feet, she encountered violent northwesterly gale force winds three miles west of Whitefish Point and went down 1½ miles offshore, amid deck icing and steering problems in an aged, leaking wooden hull. That storm claimed a half dozen ships.

The captain, Walter Neale, had ordered the crew into lifeboats, but had elected to stay with his ship.

Seeing the foundering ship, the 420-foot steel steamer Adriatic came to help by staying windward of the Myron, and the Coast Guard station at Vermilion launched a surf boat into the heavy seas to follow her. The steel freighter H. P. McIntosh came to assist by throwing lines to the sailors, but the benumbed crew could not manage to hold onto the lines. The two vessels, McIntosh and Adriatic, amid scattered lumber and shoal water, along with the Coast Guard surf boat, had to pull away.

Ironically, Captain Neale was the only survivor of the disaster; he tenaciously held onto the floating wreckage of the pilot house, which drifted free and eventually caught on the rocks of nearby Isle Parisienne. It was sighted by a passing Canadian steamer. Seeing a body she launched a lifeboat and rescued Captain Neale, half-dead from exposure. They put him in an unheated room so that he'd thaw out slowly. They figured that the slow thaw saved the captain's life.

Captain Neale later criticized the captains of the Adriatic and the McIntosh for not saving his crew.

I believe the attire of the captains of that era may have had a little bit to do with his survival. They wore heavy long-john underwear, heavy wool socks, perhaps eight-inch felt laced boots and buckled overshoes and Soo Line heavy pants made of thick (about ¼-inch) material split at the ankle about eight inches, with eyelets laced closed to eliminate drafts. Capt. Neale may have had a turtleneck woolen sweater on, and a wool shirt over that, with long, tucked-in tails; a six-foot woolen scarf wound around his neck, then a double-breasted great coat about six inches above his ankles with a large fur collar; and a pair of large gauntlet-type shearling or fur-lined gloves—all of which was topped by a fur or shearling cap, perhaps with tie-down ear flaps.

As it turned out, the pilot house wreckage Captain Neale clung to was water-washed and frozen, so he couldn't have gotten away if he had wanted to; he was frozen to the wreckage.

All 16 of his crew died by drowning or freezing, and eight bodies were eventually found the following spring by a dog team along on the southern beaches of Whitefish Bay. All were wearing their cork-filled life jackets. One guy was standing upright, frozen with his large hands over his head, as if he were climbing over the ice. "D.J." Parish, a local fisherman, found the bodies. Climbing over the ice, he and his party found a lifeboat and other bodies also frozen in the icebergs.

Men from a lumber camp returned to the beach with Parish and chopped the ice to free the bodies. The eight men were buried in a common grave at the Mission Hill Cemetery near Bay Mills, on a 400-foot hill overlooking the head waters of the St. Mary's River, between Point Iroquois and Nadoway Point.

It had taken four months to discover the bodies, but in those days it was all woods, no roads or buildings. In the spring the shore was covered with icebergs as big as houses.

The last time I visited the common grave of the sailors at Mission Hill Cemetery, it was overgrown with weeds; the small square white fence was eroded—not at all what I expected. I had thought I'd find a nice, well-kept grave site, perhaps with a bronze plaque giving an account of their drastic ordeal. Today it may be different; I hope it is.

The Myron's barge, Miztec, fared much better. She was picked up by the freighter Argus and taken to the shelter of Whitefish Point. Her rudder was gone and her deckload of lumber had been washed away.

On May 15, 1921, the Miztec sank in a snowstorm in the same area. Ironically, she had been in the tow of the steamer Zillah, whose 1st mate was Captain Neale. The Miztec's entire crew of six perished.

In 1972, divers located the Myron less than two miles west of Whitefish Point. They retrieved the anchor and donated it to the museum ship Valley Camp, situated in Sault Ste. Marie, MI. In 1982, the brass builder's plate was also found.

Captain Neale told someone that the Myron had broken in two where she had once been spliced to make her longer.

Wooden Stmr. "Myron" 186' x 28'

# The Manistique, Marquette & Northern #1 (The Milwaukee)

*T*he Manistique, Marquette & Northern #1—some name for a railroad car ferry. But she had it for only six years. She was launched in 1903, taken over by the Grand Trunk Railroad in 1909, and renamed the Milwaukee. She carried an average of 28 railroad cars across Lake Michigan, mostly from Grand Haven to Milwaukee. She ran year-round, so often had to combat heavy weather and ice, but operated for 26 years without a serious mishap—until October 22, 1929. That day she left Milwaukee with 25 railroad cars, one loaded with brand-new Nash automobiles bound for Grand Haven.

Seas were high and the full storm that struck Lake Michigan that day wrought its fury. But the ferry had encountered many similar storms in her lifetime.

This storm, however, proved to be a little different. Wind and waves were smashing on the stern when she left Milwaukee, but there the story ends, because the ship and her crew of 47 disappeared. Wreckage came ashore near Milwaukee, but the hull's whereabouts is still a mystery.

These car ferries are built with a heavy 12-foot steel gate, secured on both bottom ends like a hinge. This gate opens to form an arch, to let the box cars slide on and off the railroad car deck. A steam-operated winch lets the gate down, where it is nearly watertight.

Some time after the Milwaukee's disappearance a message container was found near South Haven Coast Guard Station. These watertight message containers are often made of brass or copper with tightly-screwed tops, so they are rustproof and waterproof. They are normally about 18 inches by 3 inches. This can was badly bent and

water did seep in. However, written in pencil was this message:
*S.S. Milwaukee, October 22nd, 6:30 P.M. —Ship is taking on water fast. We have turned and headed back for Milwaukee. Pumps are still working, but gate is bent and can't keep the water out. Flickers are flooded. Seas are tremendous. Things look bad. Crew roll about the same as last payday. Signed—A. R. Sason, Purser*

This was all that was ever heard from the vessel. "Flickers" on car-ferries are usually a couple of rooms below the main car deck and aft of the engine room for sleeping, with rest rooms, showers and perhaps a storage room.

Forty-three years later in 1972, skin divers from Milwaukee accidentally found the vessel 10 miles from Milwaukee near Wind Point. The divers did not reveal the exact spot. The wreck was on an even keel with the pilot house wrenched off and lying nearby, and the tailgate smashed. Most of the railroad cars were off the tracks at the stern of the boat, but the ones near the bow were intact and still on the tracks.

Apparently, while attempting to turn in heavy seas, the cars tore loose of their turnbuckle chain "tie-downs" and damaged the tail gate, letting water pour in. Loaded, the railroad track car deck is only about six feet above the lake level.

No one will ever know the exact reason, but it appears that's what happened. Water rushed in on deck, and the pumps couldn't begin to take care of it. All hands were lost.

Those car ferries were staunchly built.

R.R. Car-Ferry "Milwaukee" ~ 383' x 56' x 19.5'

# The Renvoyle/The Sylvania

The Canadian vessel Renvoyle was built in Scotland as a 253-foot canaler, and carried a 126-foot mid-section in her cargo hold as she crossed the Atlantic. The reason for this is that, at the time, the maximum length a boat could be to traverse the Welland Canal was 253 feet. Her final plan was to be a 379-foot vessel.

Her destination was Midland, Ontario, in the Georgian Bay, where a shipyard was to cut her in two and insert the mid-section.

The steel freighter Sylvania was launched in Bay City, MI, on March 18, 1905. She had many accidents in her life. When she was three months old she collided with the Sir Henry Bessemer off Whitefish Point on Lake Superior, putting an 80-foot hole in the Bessemer. The Sylvania was repaired in the Craig Yard in Toledo. In 1958, she was lengthened from 504 feet to 552 feet, and converted to a self unloader at the Manitowoc yard.

On June 1, 1967, while the Sylvania was unloading her cargo at the Peerless Cement Dock at Port Huron, MI, about 700 feet south of the Blue Water Bridge, the steamer Renvoyle was discharging package freight across the river at Sarnia.

Upon departing from her berth, the Renvoyle was to make a 180-degree turn and go down river. Now, the Sarnia dock is in slack water; there's no current until you're west of the dock about 300 feet, into the flow of the river, where the current is perhaps seven m.p.h. The trick is to go extremely slowly until the bow enters the river's current, then hard left and full speed. She really comes around. When she is halfway around, make a hard right to slow her and you wind up in the center of the channel.

The Renvoyle was, in my opinion, going too fast and didn't give the current a chance to set her bow clear. She plowed right into the unloading Sylvania, sinking her at the dock. Keeping the Sylvania upright were six mooring cables, each one inch in diameter) and perhaps a 3½-inch (diameter) nylon towline. There's a lot of current where she was unloading, as well as boats going by.

The Sylvania listed about 30 degrees to starboard (right). Both vessels were heavily damaged. The Sylvania was raised and towed to the repair yard in Lorain, OH.

The company surrendered the Renvoyle to the U.S. Marshall, who sold her at auction in Cleveland in a legal maneuver to limit their liability.

I used the same turning system several times to turn in that area, and the Renvoyle's captain had probably executed that same maneuver successfully at least 50 times previously.

The Renvoyle was about 42 years old, and the Sylvania about 62, at the time of the mishap. The Sylvania was 78 years old when she was finally scrapped in Ashtabula in 1968.

Ships deteriorate slowly in fresh water. My vessel, the Kinsman Independent, was 77 years old when she was scrapped—and that was because it was decided that she was too small.

I was 1st mate on the Sylvania once when we had a cargo for a sand dock in Erie, PA. After unloading, we saw the weather pick up with a strong northwesterly, so the captain had two tugs turn us toward the piers. I was on the stern watching a tug and towline—a rope three inches in diameter. The wind and current set the tug against the ship's side and the captain couldn't get away, so we threw the towline off.

I hurried to the engine room to stop the engine. I asked what direction we were heading, and they said, "ahead." I told them to wait three minutes until I got back on deck, and then to back up slowly. The towline was caught in the engine, and we might be able to pull it out this way. I had four men with me, and we pulled the line free. I informed the engineer that all was well, and called the pilot house to tell them we had no stern tug.

Normally that nylon tow line could have wrapped around the wheel and froze it. We were extremely lucky.

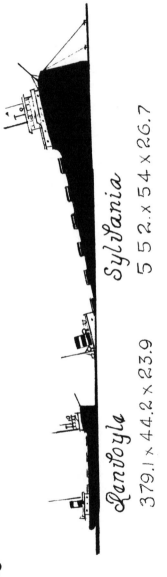

*Sylvania*

552.x 54 × 26.7

*LanToyla*

379.1 × 44.2 × 23.9

# The Arizona

The *Arizona* was launched *August 19, 1868*, in Cleveland, OH. Built with two decks and passenger cabins, she was chartered to run between Buffalo and Green Bay. In April of 1872, she changed owners and ran as a freight boat between Buffalo, Milwaukee and Chicago. In 1878 she was cut down to a single deck lumberhooker and ran in the lumber trade to Saginaw for two seasons. In 1879 she was again rebuilt, this time as a package freighter, carrying iron, general merchandise, acids, oils and kerosene upbound for the mining industry; and grain and barreled flour, downbound.

Capt. George Graser was master of the Arizona. After waiting in Marquette for two days for a violent winter storm to subside, he ventured out into a less-severe sea, only to be caught again in another storm of equal intensity. The captain turned again and headed for Marquette.

The storm grew in ferocity with violent seas that seemed to tower over the steamer's deck. Then, about five miles from Marquette's harbor, disaster struck. Some of the cargo worked loose, and a barrel of corrosive acid used for explosives began leaking. The rolling of other gear caused a spark, igniting the acid. Noxious fumes spread through the engine room, forcing the sailors to go up on deck, and leaving the engine turning full speed toward Marquette. She could be steered, but there was no way to check her speed. The crew huddled on the open deck at the bow, and luckily, the fire remained below deck, with only the smoke boiling out aft. As they approached the breakwall, the fire broke out above deck.

The captain hung onto the whistle pull, blowing the steam whistle steadily, to attract local attention and to lessen boiler steam pressure and ship speed. People were amazed to see the blazing, smoking ship roaring into the harbor. Marquette's fire alarm was sounded.

The captain steered the ship against the breakwall. It took the crew only seconds to leap onto the breakwall as the ship ground against it. She came near a stop, but—with the engines still turning at full speed—started again to pick up speed. When the crew, running ahead, noticed the blazing steamer gaining on them, they took off. The Arizona finally rammed into a slip and came to a crunching stop near the town's water works. The city's fire department and harbor tugs poured water on her all day, but her cargo of tarred building paper and chemicals only fueled the roaring blaze.

The engines continued to run, churning up mud for hours. The smokestack toppled.

In 1888, salvager Tom Reid raised the vessel and towed her to Port Huron, where she was rebuilt. Then she ran in the lumber trade for 14 years. She was again rebuilt in 1893 and given a new steeple compound engine.

Between 1902 and 1920, the Arizona changed hands three times. She ran in the lower lakes' coal and lumber trade until 1922, when she was destroyed by fire at Cape Vincent, New York. As vessels go for that era, she was a good size.

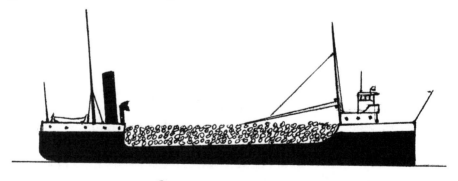

Arizona
187.3' x 32.4' x 12'

# *The David Dows*

*Schooner David Dows*

*he only five-masted sailing vessel ever built on the* Great Lakes, the David Dows, was launched April 21, 1881, at Toledo. When launched, she was the largest schooner in the world, designed to carry 140,000 bushels of grain. The main-mast was 162 feet high. She was a giant vessel that seemed to stretch out beyond reason, and proved to be almost unmanageable in the confined waters of the lakes, despite her able crew and a small steam donkey engine that was used to hoist her gigantic sails.

On September 10, about five months after her launching, in a heavy westerly squall, the crew could not handle her fast enough and she collided with the schooner Charles Nims in Lake Erie and sank her.

The owners then decided to convert the Dows to a barge. Her tall masts were shortened and a tug boat was hired to tow her around the lakes. In 1889, during a severe gale, the towing steamer Aurora cast off her tows (the David Dows and the George W. Adams). Both vessels dropped their anchors to ride out the storm off Chicago harbor in 42 feet of water. The Dows, with a cargo of iron ore, had sprung a leak, and the pumps couldn't keep up. She sank, right side up, with her masts sticking above the water. Unable to be salvaged, she was destroyed the following spring so other vessels could have free passage.

As a schooner she was huge and beautiful. Her sailing career had lasted only nine years.

# *The Tioga*

*T*he Erie Railroad Company built the Tioga in 1880. Her trade was package freight on the Great Lakes. She was 285.5 feet x 38.9 feet x 25.7 feet, and was considered fast and a nice-looking vessel. She had four white bands and three red bands on her stack.

Her first five years of operation were uneventful. But while at berth in the Chicago River in Chicago on July 11, 1885, an explosion ripped apart her stern and caused severe damage to both ship and dock. The accident killed an estimated 21 people and wreaked havoc among the ships in the nearby harbor. Huge fires spread rapidly from the explosion. The fire department was kept busy for hours, with both shore equipment and fire boats. They attributed the fire to a cargo of naphtha.

How it started was never determined, but it was the Chicago topic of discussion and law suits for many months. The ship was probed for bodies, but the explosion was so severe that many bodies were never accounted for.

The captain had had a little terrier, black and white, for about five years. This dog liked to chase the seagulls up and down the deck and to accompany the captain on his shore walks. When the ship was ready to depart and the dog was ashore, three short blasts on the steam whistle would bring him bounding back to the ship. One time the dog didn't make it, but on their return 10 days later, they saw the dog waiting on the dock.

A few said that after the 1885 mishap they saw the dog swimming away from the boat, but it was never rescued.

The Tioga was towed to the Buffalo shipyard, where she was

repaired and returned to service until 1915, when the railroads were forced to divest themselves of their package freighters. She was sold and ran until November 26, 1919, when she was stranded on Eagle Harbor Reef, on Lake Superior.

A storm raged over the lake for two days, pounding the ships that were brave enough to travel out in the fury. The Tioga hit the reef off Keweenaw Peninsula hard and stuck fast. For hours the crew huddled together, at the mercy of gale winds and giant seas. After the winds subsided and after many attempts, the crew was saved. The vessel, however, slid beneath the cold waves of Lake Superior. Her upper pilot house is a recreational building near the wreck site.

"TIOGA" 285.5' x 39' x 25.7'
1890 - 1919

# The City of Bangor

*he City of Bangor was built in Bay City in 1896. She* was 327.5 feet long. In 1905, they lengthened her to 445.5. For the next 20 years she operated in the iron ore, coal and grain trades, with few unexpected incidents to mar her career. Due to her relatively small capacity, she was sold to the Nicholson Company and was converted to an automobile carrier. They built a between-deck, halfway from her cargo hold deck and her main top deck or spar deck. Then they built elevators to lower the cars to the cargo hold deck and the 'tween-deck space. Finally they planked the main deck between the hatches, so that the deck was all the same level. She was ready for her new career: carrying new autos from Detroit to various lake ports.

Unfortunately, the City of Bangor's career as an auto carrier was short lived. On November 30, 1926, she was driven ashore on a rocky beach on the Keweenaw Peninsula in Lake Superior, near Houghton, MI. Her crew members were all able to walk ashore. The Coast Guard took them to their station to be warmed.

The vessel's port (left) side was covered with ice. The cargo of 248 brand new Chryslers suffered no more than a heavy coating of ice, and 230 of the cars were rescued from an icy grave.

A ramp was constructed, and the cars were driven off in much the same manner as they were loaded, in 15°F weather. The vessel was beyond repair, so the underwriters sold her to T. L. Durocher of DeTour, who cut her up for scrap at the site of the accident.

# The Daniel J. Morrell / The Cyprus

*The Daniel J. Morrell was built by the West* Bay City Shipbuilding Company in 1906, the standard-sized 600-footer of that era.

She gave almost 60 years of uneventful service to Bethlehem Steel Co. In 1956, she was repowered with a Skinner Uniflow Engine and radar.

On November 28, 1966, while upbound in Lake Huron in ballast, she foundered about 28 miles northeast of Harbor Beach, MI at about 2:30 a.m. in a severe gale. The ship broke in two. She could not send a distress call.

One crewman named Hall survived by pulling dead bodies over himself. His raft was picked up after a day and a half of being tossed in the heavy seas. Twenty-eight men lost their lives. This was the first vessel to sink in Lake Huron since 1924.

In an issue of the Whitefish Great Lakes Shipwreck Historical Society's newsletter, I saw another lone-survivor story, from the steamer Cyprus, which sank in a strong northwesterly storm about 15 miles east of Grand Marais and about 30 miles west of Whitefish Point.

The lone survivor was 2nd mate Charles Pitz, who relates this story: The 420-foot steel freighter was 25 days old, and carrying her second cargo of iron ore, when she encountered a fierce storm. Her hatches were not tarped and water got into her cargo hold, causing the cargo to shift. She took a strong list to port. The flooding continued until she sank. Four men got aboard a raft, but all were lost but Pitz, who hung onto the raft until it beached itself. A Deer Park Life Saving Station attendant on patrol found the mate and brought him to the station.

# The George L. Torian / The Sidney E. Smith Jr./ The Richard J. Reiss

*I found another lone-survivor marine mishap while reading* The Inland Seas. I noted that the Canadian Upper Lakes Company's vessel, the George L. Torian, 261 x 43.1 x 17.8, was torpedoed in 1941. The survivor was blown overboard and clung to a hatch cover for about 24 hours before being rescued by a passing American vessel.

The Erie Sand & Gravel Co. of Erie, PA lost its self-unloader, the Sidney E. Smith Jr., in a marine collision with a Canadian vessel, the Parker Evans, near the Blue Water Bridge in Port Huron.

The Erie company later purchased the Richard J. Reiss and decided to use the same name, but to leave off the initial— because with the initial the name had 13 letters, and might possibly bring bad luck.

Sidney E Smith Jr.

# *The Pere Marquette 18*

*he car ferry Pere Marquette 18 was launched on* August 16, 1902, in Cleveland, Ohio. The launching was a little unusual—instead of the traditional breaking of a champagne bottle on her bow, the Japanese custom of releasing a flock of doves was used.

The big car ferry, 338 x 56 x 19.5, was built for the Pere Marquette Railroad, for cross-lake service between Ludington, Kewaunee, Manitowoc and Milwaukee. She had four railroad tracks on the main deck, and 50 elegant staterooms for passengers.

The Pere Marquette 18 departed Ludington at 11:40 p.m. on September 8, 1910, eight years after her christening, bound for Milwaukee with a cargo of 29 loaded railroad cars. The wind was blowing fresh from the north; a heavy sea was running and continued to build during the night.

About 3 a.m., the oiler went aft to oil the bearings of the main shaft, which were about seven feet below the deck of the flicker, or sleeping quarters, of the engineer's crew. The oiler found the entire department full of water, and approaching the flicker room deck he went back and reported to the engineer, who called the pilot house.

The mate came back and they both went down to check. The pumps were going full, but the water was gaining. They called the captain and then tried to stop the water from coming in the deadlight (port hole), but couldn't. Everyone aboard was alerted. Three more dead lights on the port side gave 'way, admitting large quantities of water and completely filling the sleeping quarters.

In my opinion, this was crew neglect, in failing to exercise care and departing in an easy, careless manner when they all knew they had lake weather to deal with. These port holes average 12 inches in diameter, and are heavy glass, about ¾ of an inch thick. I've seen these port hole glasses crack, usually because the four evenly-spaced butterfly nuts were not equally secured tightly all the way around. Normally, in times of any approaching weather, all deadlights are checked to see that they are secure.

She started settling by the stern. In order to offset the stern weight, 12 or 13 cars were run overboard, which seemed to lighten up aft, and the crew felt easier.

At about 4:15 a.m., wireless messages were sent out for help, and life preservers passed to all aboard. Lifeboats were launched on port side (lee side). The steamer Pere Marquette 17 was sighted, distress flares were fired and the "17" closed to the "18" at about 7 a.m. Shortly afterwards, the 18 listed to starboard and started going down stern first. People began jumping overboard. The lifeboats of the 17 were lowered and 32 people were picked up; 27 lives were lost, mostly because of sea and floating wreckage. I'd say it was a miracle that so many were saved. In open lifeboats and roaring seas, they did well to save as many as they did.

The exact cause of the sinking could not be determined, because all the officers of the ship were lost, and none of the 32 rescued knew why the Pere Marquette 18 had foundered. Experts guessed they may have had a fractured stern tube, or a broken stern tube gland, or perhaps a bulkhead gave way. But they won't ever really know. It was somewhat similar to the foundering of the Edmund Fitzgerald. She was only 14 miles from Whitefish Point, and shelter.

# The Chicora

*he wooden passenger and freight steamer Chicora* was launched in Detroit June 25, 1892, to carry passengers to Lake Michigan ports, and fruit and vegetables back to Chicago and Milwaukee. She was 198.5 feet long, 35 feet wide and 13.6 feet deep, a smart propeller vessel and capable of 16 knots.

Late in December of 1894, after she was laid up for winter, the shippers asked that she make one more trip, carrying bagged flour from Milwaukee to Benton Harbor, and then return for winter layup.

On January 21, at 5 a.m., the vessel cleared Milwaukee. A winter storm was brewing, the barometer had been falling steadily all the previous day, but the captain and crew were eager to complete the trip and return to their homes.

Pounded by ice and tossed like a cork by the great waves, the Chicora fought the storm for hours that afternoon and finally lost the fight and sank. She was never seen again. She carried 23 crew members and one passenger to their deaths somewhere in Lake Michigan's icy waters. Rescue crews spent days looking for her, but to no avail.

Captain Henry F. Stines of the steamer City of Ludington spent two days looking for his brother, Captain Eddie Stines, on the Chicora, but found no trace of the vessel or crew after the storm. Later that year, bags of flour, parts of the ship, her name board, and her mast, washed ashore near Saugatuck, MI.

The mast now stands at Glenn Lake, MI, as a sad reminder of the proud Chicora and her crew.

# The Perry G. Walker / The Crescent City

*T*he *Perry G. Walker* was built in 1903, and was 416 feet x 50.3 feet x 24 feet. This ship was involved in one of the most peculiar incidents ever to happen on the Great Lakes.

On June 9, 1909, the Walker was west-bound at Sault Ste. Marie. Because of heavy traffic, she decided to take the Canadian Lock. The Canadian passenger steamer Assiniboia was tied up at the east end of the lock, and the steamer Crescent City was tied up behind her, both downbound and waiting to be locked through.

The lock was filled with water. The Walker, upbound, was approaching the tie-up wall, to await the departure of the downbound boats in the lock.

As the Walker approached, she signaled the engineer for "dead slow." There was a mix-up, and the Walker bolted ahead, smashing down the lock gate and knocking it off its hinges. The lock's full head of water came tumbling out, carrying the Assiniboia and the Crescent City with it. The Assiniboia somehow miraculously escaped hitting the Walker, and plummeted into lower St. Mary's River. The steamer Crescent City, following closely behind, could not keep control and followed the passenger ship in hot pursuit through the open lock.

Here again a miracle occurred, for the Crescent City, loaded with iron ore, scraped the lock's cement bottom, doing a great deal of damage to the bottom of the ship. However, her pumps were able to control the water, and she proceeded on to her unloading port in Ohio.

The entire incident took only a few minutes. The passengers on the Assiniboia were roughed up, but unhurt. The Canadian lock was soon repaired. The Assiniboia and the Walker sustained only minor damage. But the unlucky Crescent City spent the winter in the shipyard for the second time in two years. She had been caught in a terrific storm in 1905 and had landed on a rocky shore.

The Crescent City was sold to Interlake, renamed Taurus, and ran without incident until 1947, when she was sold for scrap and cut up in Hamilton, Ontario, near Toronto.

Perry G. Walker - 1903

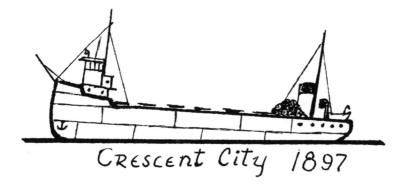

Crescent City 1897

# The E. W. Oglesby

Steamer *E. W. Oglesby was launched May 16, 1896, at* Bay City, MI. She was 375.6 x 45.8 x 23.2.

In 1922, Captain Charles H. Mohr, then 45 and captain of the E. W. Oglesby, rescued two men, two women and three children from a sinking yacht in Lake Huron's Georgian Bay near Tobermory, Ontario.

On her 31st year, December 8, 1927, sailing in ballast (no cargo) for Fort William, Ontario, with winds more than 50 miles per hour, she stranded at 5:30 p.m. on Shot Point, about 10 miles from Marquette. She caught fire, putting the crew in double peril.

Fortunately, the Coast Guard was able to get a tug to the stricken vessel. The fish tug Columbia also arrived at the scene. The entire crew was removed by the Coast Guard, transferred to the tug and taken to Marquette for safety.

The hull was stripped and left there for the winter. She was purchased by T. L. Durocher Towing of DeTour, MI. A year and four months later she was released and taken to Drummond Island, MI. In 1930, her cabins were removed and the vessel sunk as part of a dock for the Drummond Island Dolomite Co. There she remains, while today's vessels tie up to load stone at the plant.

Capt. Mohr was credited with saving the lives of 27 men, women and children in five different rescues over a 10-year span. He died in Florida in 1943, and was buried in Montague, MI.

# The Sport

*I*n 1872 Wyandotte Shipyard launched the lakes' first steel-hulled vessel, the small tug Sport, valued at approximately $21,000.

In 1913, a great November storm sank or totally destroyed 19 ships and claimed 250 lives. A capsized freighter was discovered 13 miles north of Port Huron on November 11. Three days later, the Sport reached the wreck, remained there overnight, and the next morning sent a diver down and found the words "Charles S. Price." They returned to Port Huron and revealed the mystery ship's name.

The Sport's final voyage began on December 13, 1920, when she was 48 years old. She departed Port Huron with a crew of six men en route to Harbor Beach to pick up a barge. The wind was easterly and picking up. About 6 p.m. the engineer called the captain, saying that she was taking on more water than the pumps could handle. They launched a lifeboat and abandoned the sinking tug. After a three-hour ordeal, they were swept ashore at Lexington, MI, about 25 miles north of Port Huron. Before leaving the vessel, the captain tied a buoy to a long rope, but the following morning the buoy was gone.

The Sport lay there for 67 years before being found on June 10, 1987, in 47 feet of water. The Michigan Historical Commission placed a marker near the Sport's sunken remains. Today the Sport is a popular recreational diving site.

# The Senator

On June 20, 1896, the Senator was launched. She was a steel vessel measuring 410 x 45.4 x 23.9, and was for her day considered a large vessel. Her pilot house was set quite a distance aft (back) from her stem, and she had one hatch forward from her pilot house. Later on in her auto-carrying career, the pilot house was moved forward near the stem.

During her career she had 10 different owners, the last of whom in 1929 was Nicholson of Detroit, and she carried autos at that time.

In 1927, the captain's daughter Mary Ann and her kitten Missy rode the boat all summer. She liked it so well, he made her a porter for the next two years.

The Senator was almost lost on August 22, 1909, when the Norman B. Ream struck her in the St. Mary's River near Pipe Island in dense fog. She sank almost immediately, but lay submerged with her spars above water. She was raised, repaired and returned to service.

On October 31, 1929, with a load of automobiles, she collided with the steamer Marquette off Port Washington, WI, in thick fog and sank, taking 20 of her 29-man crew with her. The Marquette picked up nine of the crew, among them the captain and Mary Ann, but the little cat was lost.

~ Senator ~

# The T. L. Durocher (Lt. Col. Lawrence O. Matthews)

The steel tug *T.L. Durocher* was launched September 22, 1930, during the Depression, for the Durocher Salvage Company in DeTour Village, MI. Unfortunately the economy continued to be bad, and Mr. Durocher could not meet his payments. The tug was repossessed by the American Ship Building Co. and lay idle most of the time. It was chartered only twice in six years.

In 1941, the U.S. Army purchased the tug and renamed her Lt. Col. Lawrence O. Matthews, and she was then used to tow barges around northern Quebec. On October 28, 1942, at the south end of Ungava Bay on the Koksoak River, the big tug was lost in a severe storm. The Tug Durocher was a beautiful, large, powerful tug. I am sure Mr. Durocher never really got over losing it.

## TUG T.L. DUROCHER
## 117.5' X 28.2' X 14.9'

# The William C. Moreland

ere is an unusual *Great Lakes* story about the steamer William C. Moreland. The steel bulk freighter was launched July 26, 1910, at Lorain, OH. On October 18, on her fifth trip, with a cargo of 10,700 tons of iron ore, she became stranded in a storm on the Sawtooth Reef at Eagle Harbor, MI.

Wreckers were immediately dispatched, but heavy weather prevented any work. On November 2, they succeeded in removing part of her cargo, but severe weather set in and the ship was abandoned and broke into three parts. The center section was hard on the rocks and the bow was over deep water. She broke at hatches 12 and 24. Winter set in.

In the spring another storm sank the bow section. The center section was beyond salvage; the stern was all that was left. This was bulkheaded with a cofferdam and floated off the reef on August 8, 1911. It was towed to Portage Harbor in the Keweenaw waterway, boarded up and left for the winter. The next year the 254-foot stern section was towed to Port Huron and then to Ecorse, and finally across the river to Windsor, Ontario, in November of 1912.

Due to increased steel prices and high costs for new ships, as well as the demand for tonnage during World War I, Roy M. Wolvin of Duluth bought her. In 1916, she was towed to Superior, WI and on September 16th of that year a new 346-foot front section was tacked on—and the new freighter, Sir Trevor Dawson, entered service. She was renamed three more times: Charles L. Hutchinson; Gene C. Hutchinson; and finally, Parkdale, for a Canadian company, where she carried coal and grain.

On May 12, 1970, she was sold to Spain for scrap. She and

another ship, the Alexander Leslie, were towed in tandem and arrived in Spain June 8, 1970.

So after 60 years, the stern section wound up in Spain while the bow section was still sleeping in Lake Superior. She had been an all-steel ship 580 feet long, 58 feet wide and 32 feet deep.

She had foundered after only 81 days.

*- 1910 - William C. Moreland -*

# The George M. Humphrey (The Adam E. Cornelius)

On June 15, 1943, the steamer George M. Humphrey was Chicago-bound in dense fog with 14,000 tons of iron ore when she collided with the D.M. Clemson in the Straits of Mackinac, 1½ miles northeast of Mackinaw City. The collision ripped a hole 18 feet by 22 feet in the Humphrey's starboard side, near the #3 hatch.

She went down in 80 feet of water with no loss of life. The insurance company wrote her off as a total loss. She had been the flagship of the Kinsman Transit Company, owned by the Steinbrenner family. At this time (1996) the company is still operating two grain vessels, with a third boat on standby.

Captain John Roen of Sturgeon Bay put in his bid: he'd either raise her and salvage her, or destroy her, so she wouldn't be a menace to navigation. This was distinctly a million-dollar gamble. If he raised her, she'd be his and worth $1,000,000. There were no competitive bids, and most vessel operators were skeptical.

Capt. Roen was from Norway, and was self-educated. As a young man he had once worked on the Chief Wawatam, a railroad ferry.

Salvage operations started on October 20, and by November 6 hatch markers were towed to the wreck. Despite foul weather, work proceeded for 49 days, until heavy ice sealed her for the winter. Before that, a clam bucket from Roen's barge, the Maitland, a former Lake Michigan car ferry, had brought up 8,000 tons of iron ore, along with a plan to raise her. On May 6 they were back to work.

Divers removed 300 1¼-inch rivets from her gunwale bar, which is the top of her hull plating on both sides, the full length of her deck. In place of the rivets they put 50 equally-spaced rings, through which they wove some 2½ miles of continuous cable, and mating sheaves attached to the sides of the barge Maitland, which was anchored directly over the Humphrey. This cable had to be continuous in order to provide self-adjustment of tension when hoisting began. In reality, it would be similar to lacing a boot, but with the eyelets 80 feet apart. Additional bow and stern lines were added to both vessels.

The Maitland took on full water ballast to sink her to a draft of 17 feet. Then, with tension on the lifting cables, the Humphrey's tanks were pumped out to raise the Humphrey seven feet off the bottom. Then they towed her, ever so slowly, until she settled on the bottom again. Then they pumped water again into the barge's tanks and tightened up on the tension cables. Five times in the first mile and a half, they repeated this procedure, each time lifting her seven feet nearer the water's surface.

When there was no longer clearance between the Humphrey's superstructure and the barge, the secured two barges drew parallel with the Humphrey's ship sides so she could be raised exactly between the two barges. The cables were then re-rigged so that the Humphrey could be raised between them. The carefully-equalized job of slowly lifting and sledding the sunken craft, with the two barges acting as pontoons, finally brought the Humphrey to rest with her hatches clear of the water's surface.

On September 8 the water was pumped out of her hold. Divers plugged her leaks and a timber patch was built over the gaping hole in her side. On Sept 10 the Humphrey was finally floated; on September 17 she was in tow to Sturgeon Bay. The U. S. Corps of Engineers said this feat was unparalleled in maritime history.

She came out as the Captain John Roen, and ran a couple of years before being sold to Boland, also known as the American Steamship Company, with the understanding that her name could never be changed. However, Boland converted her to a self-unloader and, because of the change in structure, could then rename her the Adam E. Cornelius.

# The Roy A. Jodrey

## M.V. Roy A. Jodrey

he Roy A. Jodrey, a modern steel diesel 620-foot self-unloader, was launched in 1965 for the Algoma Central Railroad of Sault Ste. Marie, Ontario, as part of its fleet modernization and expansion program.

On November 21, 1974, the nine-year-old vessel, while upbound with ore from Sept Isles, Quebec, to Detroit, veered off course in the Alexandria Bay Narrows in the St. Lawrence River and collided with buoy #194. She then ran aground on Pullman Light Shoal. (There's a Pullman Castle in that area, a really beautiful building.)

The Jodrey began taking on water and developing a list. Five hours later, this big, modern self-unloader slipped off the shoal and sank in 200 feet of water. All 29 crew members had been taken off by the Coast Guard.

After surveys, the underwriters figured salvage was impossible and the Jodrey was declared a total loss. I don't know, of course, but I believe if that mishap occurred today they'd figure a way to salvage her. I believe one of their great problems would be the swift current in that area.

Then again, at one time the face of Niagara Falls was eroding. They dammed the river above the falls, kept the falls damp with hoses, and installed a heavy iron strap across the top of the falls. While they were doing that, the tourist attraction was great. To see that water roaring over the falls, one would think that it would be impossible to shift that water to the Canadian falls. In my opinion, some seemingly impossible projects are possible.

# The Omar D. Conger

## OMAR D. CONGER ~

O mar D. Conger was a passenger ferry between Port Huron, MI, and Sarnia, Ontario. This 92-foot wooden ferry was launched May 2, 1882, on the Black River in Port Huron. She is so well-remembered because she affected many lives in that area. A steady ferry boat, she also participated in many excursion runs.

After a fire that burned and charred her and destroyed her upper works in 1901, she was rebuilt and renamed the City of Port Huron. A new engine was also installed. Twenty-one years later, at 2:22 p.m., while her captain was returning to his ship to get ready for the 3:00 run, she was rocked by an explosion that shook houses and sent people scurrying about in wonderment. Four members of her crew, the chief engineer, fireman and two deckhands were killed.

The explosion not only sank and completely devastated the vessel, but hurled a 125-pound boiler valve through the roof of a store and sent a 200-pound radiator crashing into a funeral parlor. It also blew parts of the boiler into a nearby house, smashing it into rubble. A lifeboat davit pierced the corner of a brick building, entering one side and protruding from the other like a curved sail needle. The violent explosion was blamed on lack of water in the boiler—human error.

A nearby ferry, the Hiawatha, was badly damaged in dock, and the other ferry, City of Cheboygan, was rocked as it entered the river.

Only chance and timing saved scores of people. At that time there were many ferries of that size, and because the boats were wooden there were many fires.

# *The Margaret Olwill*

O*n June 29, 1899, the steam barge Margaret Olwill loaded* limestone at Kelly Island, which is near Sandusky, OH. She left at midnight bound for Cleveland. This was usually an uneventful run, but at 4:30 a.m. on the 30th when abeam of Lorain, and about eight miles offshore, the wheel chains parted. The wind being fresh northeast, the Olwill fell off in the trough of the sea and rolled hard, rolling the cabin houses off. Part of the crew got away in a lifeboat, which capsized. The Olwill foundered about 6 a.m.

The steamers State of Ohio and Sacramento picked up four of her crew. Later in the morning the tug Cascade, under the command of Capt. James F. Bowen, picked up three more men from the wreckage. Captain Brown, his wife and two children, with four crew members, were drowned. Later most of the bodies washed up on the beach east of Vermilion, OH. Considerable wreckage came ashore at Cedar Point. The brother of Captain Brown, George, was in command of the steamer Arrow when he sighted the wreckage. Among it was the nameboard off the Olwill pilot house.

Tragedy had struck again, as it had so many times. When relatives sailed the lakes, multiple deaths brought anxiety and sorrow to many households.

In later years, members of the same immediate family were not permitted to be hired on the same vessel because of what happened on the Margaret Olwill. It is a great tragedy to lose even one member of a household, not to mention the deaths of an entire family. Even though the frequency of sinkings has diminished these days, the rule is still observed. However, unless my memory fails me, a Sullivan family had seven brothers on a Navy ship and the ship was lost, all brothers perishing. Seems to me the Navy later named a ship in honor of that family: The Sullivan Brothers. I believe further that the vessel is a museum in Buffalo harbor today. I remember that a green shamrock was painted on the pilot house.

~THE HARVESTER~
525 x 58 x 31

# *The City of Everett*

*I*n 1894, the whaleback steamer City of Everett was launched. "Launched" is an understatement, as she had to be moved five miles on rollers from the building site to the launching site. In the meantime her engines were being built at Frontier Iron Works in Detroit, 2,000 miles away. She was 346 x 42.1 x 22.9, with 2,595 gross tonnage and 2,300 horsepower.

A whaleback steamer is built like a huge cigar, with about a third of her width flattened out, and hatches installed for her cargo hold. Shipbuilder Alexander McDougall had a dream one night of a freighter built like a huge cigar with hatches along her top. In the dream it was stormy and the seas were rolling right off her. McDougall built a total of 39 such vessels, and these plied the lakes for some 70 years. Some of them became tankers, a few passenger ships, and the rest general cargo vessels. A few large barges were also constructed, but as time went on and more modern ways of unloading were conceived, her hatches were becoming a problem, as the unloading was too large a job for her small hatches.

The whalebacks became known as "pigs," and served well as oil tankers. One, the tanker Meteor, originally the ore carrier Frank Rockefeller, became a land-locked museum in the yacht harbor of Superior, WI.

On a trip to New York the City of Everett went to the aid of steamer Adriatic, disabled and sinking off Nantucket. The dignity of the Adriatic was offended and her captain refused to be towed by a lowly pigboat.

The City of Everett, however, stood by for 24 hours until the revenue cutter arrived to tow the Adriatic into port. By then, though, it was too late. The liner sank. The captain of the City of Everett was sure he could have saved her.

The City of Everett was one of a kind. When loaded she had practically no free board. At one time a captain erroneously reported her sinking when the seas were flush with her deck.

Her demise came in 1923 when, with a cargo of molasses, she got caught in a hurricane off American Shoals, FL, and was lost with all hands.

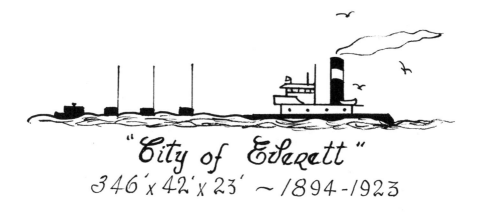

"City of Everett"
346' x 42' x 23' ~ 1894-1923

# The "85"/The Admiral

McDougall of Superior built a steel tank barge in 1913 for Standard Oil Company. This barge had several names, but the number "85" seems to have stuck with her. For example, S.O. 85, L.T. Co. 85, Socony 85, Gotham 85, and finally Cleveco 85 in 1940. But she had only operated about a year under that last name when she had her mishap.

Towed by Cleveland Tankers' tug Admiral, she departed Toledo bound for Cleveland on December 2, 1940. Then they ran into a severe storm. The details of their last flight are not clear, as no one was saved to explain. Both the tug and barge disappeared with all hands. There had been 11 men on the barge and seven on the tug. The whereabouts of the tug was unknown until 1967, when skin divers happened to find her.

Because of the shallowness of the water and closeness to the lake shipping lanes, she was raised and towed to deeper water and was allowed to sink again. The value of scrapping the old tanker was minimal. Oddly, she had been 27 years old when she sank, and she lay on the bottom for 27 years before being found.

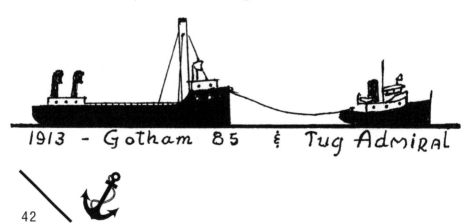

1913 - Gotham 85 & Tug Admiral

# The Western Reserve / The W. H. Gilcher

*I*n 1890, two identical steel vessels were launched in Cleveland, both 301.5 feet in length, 41.2 feet in breadth and 21.1 feet depth. These two, the W. H. Gilcher and the Western Reserve, were good-sized vessels in their day, and competed for top carrying records during the seasons 1891 and 1892. Their company was the Minch Steamship Company, which is now Steinbrenner's Kinsman Company.

In 1892, Captain Peter Minch, his wife, daughter and 10-year-old son, along with Mrs. Minch's sister and her daughter, climbed aboard the Western Reserve at Cleveland for a combination pleasure and business trip to Two Harbors, MN. The vessel was in ballast and was to pick up a cargo of iron ore.

Between Cleveland and Whitefish Bay the trip was uneventful. The captain anchored at Whitefish to study the weather. The wind and seas showed no signs of increasing, so he decided to hove anchor and press on. Late in the evening of August 30, the vessel rode into a full gale. Shortly afterwards a loud crack was heard and a fissure appeared on deck ahead of the boiler house. This crack began to widen, and with the continual pounding, the ship took in the now-heavy seas.

Suddenly, with a deafening roar, the vessel broke in two and within two minutes slipped beneath the waves.

A metal lifeboat and wooden yawl managed to survive the plunge of the sinking ship, and all of the crew of 21 and the six passengers scrambled aboard. The wooden yawl held 18, the metal boat nine. Five of the crew went down with the ship. Then it was discovered that the metal boat was in a sinking condition. As the people in the wooden yawl tried to transfer the others into their already crowded boat, only two, the youngest and a man, made it.

The wooden yawl managed to survive for a period of time until it turned over and was engulfed by the waves. The boy's strength ebbed quickly and he, too, disappeared in the waves.

The seaman, Harry Stewart, managed to reach shore, where he lay exhausted. Finally he was able to walk 10 miles to the Deer Park Life-Saving Station, where he told his story. The bodies of 16 people eventually washed ashore, including four of the Minch family. The yawl reached the shore outside of Grand Marais, MI.

Just a few months later, the Western Reserve's near sister suffered a similar, but more mysterious, fate. In the fall of 1892, the Gilcher departed Buffalo, NY with 3,000 tons of coal cargo, bound for Milwaukee, WI. A severe gale lashed Lake Michigan on the 28th of October, just as the Gilcher left the Straits of Mackinac and headed into the fury of the storm.

The Gilcher, with all 18 hands, vanished from the face of the angry lake. The storm continued for several days, and on November 4th wreckage from two vessels washed ashore on High Island. Pieces of wreckage were found bearing the names "W. H. Gilcher" and the wooden schooner "Ostrich." The Ostrich had a cargo of hemlock timber and a crew of seven. She had been under the command of her owner, Captain John McKay. No bodies were ever recovered. Both ships had simply vanished with all hands during the severe weather conditions.

The post mortems about the fate of the W. H. Gilcher and the Western Reserve were begun by masters, crewmen, shipbuilding firms, owners, insurance under-writers and historians. To this day, the reason the Gilcher disappeared is unknown—collision, structural steel failure, ship design, safety infraction or navigational hazards.

We'll just never know. But after the sinking of the Western Reserve and its near sister, the W. H. Gilcher, it was determined that the steel structure used in these vessels was brittle. After that, close attention was paid to the tempering of steel used in shipbuilding so that vessels could withstand twisting and pounding without cracking.

In my time, aboard vessels in storms, I've often noticed the after cabins twisting to the right, and the forward cabins twisting to the left, and the midship section heaving up and down and taking heavy rolling seas over the deck at the same time.

Up to the time vessels reached 600 feet in length, they were required to carry a lifeline stretching from the forward cabins to the after cabins and about eight feet above deck at its lowest point. This line was a steel cable with about 20 iron rings attached, 10 aft and 10 forward. Attached to these rings were lengths of one-inch rope. In heavy weather, when an occasional sea would break on deck, we were required to walk the deck assisted by holding on to one of these lines. Running in ballast, we did not use the lines, as the vessel rode high in the water.

In heavy weather, if possible, we checked the vessel's speed and tried to head into or near into the coming seas. The vessel will ride more comfortably and not take near the pounding this way. Most of the time, of course, it would depend on our location and direction. If we had lake room, we'd take advantage of our direction.

If you're in a violent storm, you are much more frightened, worried about hanging on, than you are about being seasick. Of course, all of us sailors have been scared at one time or another, whether we admitted it or not.

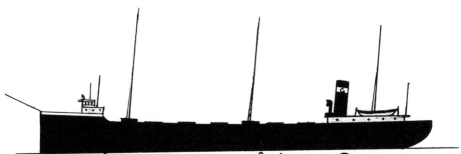

The W.H. Gilcher & Western Reserve

# The Thomas W. Palmer / The Harvard

On May 16, 1905, the steamer *Thomas W. Palmer* was upbound with a cargo of coal bound for Duluth. The steamer Harvard was downbound with a cargo of iron ore, in dense, heavy fog, when the two vessels collided off Standard Rock, about 45 miles east of Copper Harbor, MI, in about 600 feet of water. Quick thinking on the part of both skippers saved the Palmer's entire crew of 19 men. The captain of the ill-fated Palmer called to the captain of the Harvard to keep his bow pinned in the Palmer's side until he could get his crew onto the Harvard. This he did, and the entire crew quickly moved to the other boat.

The Harvard had struck the Palmer between the second and third hatches on the starboard side. When the Harvard backed off, the water rushed into the great hold and the Palmer started to sink, bow first. As she settled lower the tremendous rush of water set her whistles off. It was as if she was blowing a final salute or farewell. It was all over in a few minutes. It was a great loss and a personal one for the Palmer's master. He had been captain on her for 15 years since she first went in service in 1889.

There was some concern at first that the Harvard would sink also. Her bow was badly crushed and she was taking on water. Because of that concern, they transferred the Palmer's crew to a passing steamer, the G. Watson (French), which took them to Detroit. At the Sault they inspected the Harvard and finally allowed her to proceed to her unloading dock.

# The Azov

*I*n 1866 William Buntin of Wellington Square, Ontario, had the two-masted schooner Azov built for himself. She was 180.4 x 23.7 x 10, and had nice lines. She ran mostly in the salt and lumber trade on Lake Huron and Georgian Bay for her first 20 years. In 1906, Captain John McDonald sold his schooner, the John G. Kolfage, in order to purchase the Azov and have it rebuilt at Sarnia, Ontario.

Sailing the Azov on Lake Huron became a family affair. Captain McDonald's son Dan was mate, and his daughter Elita was in charge of the galley. The McDonalds painted their attractive schooner white with green trim and white sails.

On October 22, 1911, she was southbound on Lake Huron loaded with lumber and shingles for Chatham, Ontario. She was working her way across the mouth of Saginaw Bay in heavy weather when she began to leak. The crew exhausted themselves at the pumps and the Azov began to settle, becoming unmanageable.

The yawl was lowered and the crew abandoned the boat, east by south, nine miles from Pointe aux Barques. The empty schooner quickly broached to and capsized. Capt. McDonald, his crew of five and his son and daughter were driven away from the Michigan shore by westerly winds. They rowed and bailed as the little yawl sailed across the heaving lake. (A yawl is like a rowboat: no cabins, exposed to the weather.) Sometimes the waves roared over them and half-filled the little boat.

Crew members were in a state of exhaustion, cold and wet, and all became drowsy. The captain had to prod them occasionally to keep them going. Eighteen hours and 45 miles later, they came ashore six miles north of Goderich, Ontario. A farmer took them to his house, where they all recovered sufficiently to make the stagecoach trip to Goderich. They were surely one happy group to have survived that ordeal.

The Azov drifted across the lake and was found by the tug McGaw five miles off Kincardine. An attempt was made to tow her, but she would not follow. She eventually came ashore near McGregor Point, four miles south of Port Elgin. The elements broke her to pieces.

*Schooner Azov*
*Length 108.4 Beam 23.7 Depth 10.0*

# 𝒯he 𝐵en 𝐸. 𝒯ate /
# Our 𝒮on

𝓜y first permanent command was the self-unloader Ben E. Tate, which was 356 x 50 x 24. Before my time, on her first season as a self-unloader in 1930, there was a gale during the night of September 25 in mid-Lake Michigan. The gale tore the sails of the last lake-built sailing vessel still in commercial operation, the 55-year-old schooner Our Son, leaving her helpless.

Because of high seas it was impossible to launch her yawl, so her 73-year-old master was at the mercy of the sea. To the north at dawn on the 26th, the captain on the Tate chose to run down the storm-tossed east shore of Lake Michigan instead of running to the lee west shore, and on down to Chicago. Weather was westerly and building when, off Ludington, for some unknown reason, he changed course again, due west for the west shore.

The Tate took a real beating and her cabins were damaged, but she plowed on. At about 3 p.m. the Tate spied the schooner Our Son in the trough of the sea, taking a terrific beating. The Tate sent a radio call for help. The Pere Marquette #22 answered and said she was on the way, but the Tate decided he couldn't wait for the car ferry and proceeded on to help the sailboat. They poured storm oil on the waters to flatten the sea somewhat, and brought her alongside the sailboat long enough for her captain and six-man crew to leap aboard the Tate.

The schooner sank a short time later. The Tate arrived safely at South Chicago and was greeted by a cheering crowd. The Ben E. Tate's Captain Charles H. Mohr was later awarded a Congressional Medal of Honor for what was termed "one of the most daring pieces of expert seamanship in the history of navigation."

In 1954, the Columbia Steamship Company bought the Ben E. Tate. I was her captain in 1964, and on July 12, 1968, she was towed to a scrap dock in Balboa, Spain to be scrapped.

Normally a lake freighter width is about ⅒ of her length. The Tate's length was 356 feet and her width was 50 feet, so she was exceptionally "beamy" for her length.

Stmr. Ben E Tate
356' x 50 x 24

Schooner Our Son
106' x 25.4' x 9.9

# The 1940
# Armistice Day Disaster

*I*n 1937, wanting to become a mate, I quit the state ferries to take a job on the iron ore lake freighters. My first boat was 450 x 50, the Cygnus. When I first went aboard her, I thought she was huge.

Three of us shared a room—John, Walter and I. We never shared a boat after that, but we always kept in touch. John got the first wheeling job and I got the second. I was wheeling on the Augustus B. Wolvin in November of 1940, when we met Walter's boat downbound at St. Clair, MI. He yelled over that he was getting off and going wheeling on the William B. Davock en route for Chicago. I yelled back, "Good for you, Walter, and good luck!" We were about eight hours ahead of the Davock en route to Duluth.

On the Davock Walter hooked up with two other vessels, the Novadoc and the Anna C. Minch in the Straits area, and the three of them headed down Lake Michigan for Chicago. They ran into a terrific storm off Pentwater, MI, near Ludington, and all three vessels perished. The Davock lost 32 men, 27 from the Minch and one from the Novadoc, for a total of 60.

Three brothers owned the 25-foot wooden fishing tug Three Brothers, a black tug trimmed in red and docked in Ludington harbor. The Coast Guard issued warnings that no boat should attempt to rescue the men from these imperiled ships, as too many had already perished and they did not want to have to add to the list.

However, the Three Brothers made two attempts to depart and were driven back. The third attempt was successful, and they managed to rescue all of the Novadoc's crew (who had been all huddled together at the bow of the ship when found) but one who had washed over the side.

The other two vessels were not so fortunate. They both sank with all hands. After the storm, bodies were found on the beach, some of them with lifejackets from the other ship on. That made some people believe that the two ships may have gotten together, but no one will ever know for sure.

A few days later, the Coast Guard was going to sue the Three Brothers for going against their orders. However, the newspapers got hold of the story and the Coast Guard pulled in their horns.

As a rule, November is the worst month of the year for lake storms.

Some time later I recall putting on a gray dress shirt and happened to look inside the collar. There, stamped on the shirt, was The name of Walter Kewise, my buddy who went down on the Davock. We used to swap clothes, and I wound up with his shirt. Walter, I am sure, would have eventually made captain.

The Three Brothers was just found on the bottom of Lake Superior in 1996.

The Chicago-bound Harvester was the last to see those three vessels. The captain looked ahead, and saw a huge high wave, called a seiche,* stretching from east to west and heading north, bound straight for them. He estimated the seiche to be about 40 feet high with white foam stretching its length. The captain called the chief and told him, "There's a huge wave coming at us. If we can get through it, I think we'll be okay." He checked the boat's speed and told the chief, "Keep the steam right up there, and just before we strike that wave we'll ring up for full speed. That way we'll have good steerage." That's what they did, and they came through all right. However, when the wave struck, it came right over the pilot house and rolled down on the canvas-tarped hatches and on aft, where it struck the after cabins, rolling on over the top of the cabins, taking the large ventilators with it as well as one of the lifeboats.

The cook had been cooking donuts with the skylight open for air. The engine room also had its skylight open for air, and as the wave passed over it a few donuts dropped into the engine room.

Ironically, after the captain managed to navigate the Harvester through that terrific storm, the company fired him a year later for drinking. He had been an excellent ship-handler; but with some large companies, you're just a number.

Although I was never a rough drinking man, I felt bad when that captain was fired.

The Harvester went on to Chicago and was in the shipyard all winter. In 1946, I was 2nd mate on her, and in about 1972, I was her captain. By that time her name had been changed to Chicago Trader. She has now been scrapped.

During that 1940 Armistice Day storm when I was on the Augustus B. Wolvin, I believe we were en route to Duluth, but anchored behind Whitefish Point.

I still think about that storm occasionally.

"Stmr. Wm. B. Davock"
420' x 52' x 23'
Cable above deck, with Rope Rings, used in storms

* (Webster: seiche: an oscillation of the surface of a lake or land-locked sea that varies in period from a few minutes to several hours.)

# The William F. Sauber

## William F. Sauber ~ 291' x 41' x 19.8'

*T*he steamer *William F. Sauber,* 291 x 41 x 19.8, was built in 1891 in Bay City, MI. She was a wooden bulk freighter built for the ore trade. At that time she was considered a good-sized boat.

On October 24, 1903, she departed Ashland, WI with a cargo of iron ore bound for a Lake Erie port. About 300 miles later, off Keweenaw Point, the steamer ran into a severe gale in the vicinity of Manitou Island. She sprang a leak and water gained steadily on the pumps. The following day at nightfall, they figured the Sauber was in great peril. Signals of distress were displayed and the steamer Yale came to assist her.

The Yale positioned herself close and to the windward side of the Sauber. Slowly the vessels crept to the safety of Whitefish Point. By 11 p.m. on the 25th it became obvious that the wooden freighter wasn't going to make it. The captain of the Yale brought his vessel as close to the Sauber as he could and the Sauber crew began the four-hour process of abandoning ship.

Captain Morris, master of the Sauber, ordered his crew to take to the yawls and go over to the Yale. He chose to stay with his vessel. When the cold water hit the red-hot boilers, she blew up and sank immediately. Captain Morris was observed floating among the wreckage and crying for help. A line was thrown to him, but benumbed with cold, he was unable to grasp it. He perished in the sight of help. His little dog was seen swimming near him, but also didn't make it.

The Sauber sank October 26, 30 miles off the safety of Whitefish Point. The Yale took the 15 survivors to the Sault, where they were cared for and sent home.

**II**

# *Personal Shipping Stories*

*Keep her in the middle of the stream—*

SERIAL NUMBER 641347

UNITED STATES COAST GUARD

FILE NO.

ISSUE NUMBER 10 - 11

LICENSE

TO U.S. MERCHANT MARINE OFFICER

*This is to certify that* * * * RAY I. MCGRATH * * * *
*having been duly examined and found competent by the undersigned, is licensed to serve as* MASTER OF GREAT LAKES OR
INLAND STEAM OR MOTOR VESSELS OF ANY GROSS TONS, NOT INCLUDING WATERS
GOVERNED SOLELY BY INTERNATIONAL REGULATIONS FOR THE PREVENTION OF
COLLISION AT SEA, 1972; ALSO, FIRST CLASS PILOT ON VESSELS OF ANY GROSS
TONS UPON THE GREAT LAKES BETWEEN DULUTH, GARY, BUFFALO, NORTH TONAWANDA
AND OGDENSBURG. * * * * * * * * * * * * * * * * * * * * * * * * * * * *
* * RADAR OBSERVER (UNLIMITED) – ENDORSEMENT EXPIRES FEBRUARY 1995. * *
*for the term of five years from this date.*

*Given under my hand this* 25TH *day of* JUNE 19 90.
THIS LICENSE REPLACES LICENSE NUMBER 577747 ISSUED AT TOLEDO, OHIO ON THE DATE ABOVE.

TOLEDO, OHIO 4/27/92
*Port*

C. D. KAKUSKA, LCDR., U.S.C.G.
*Officer in Charge of Marine Inspection*

By Dir.

Bureau of Engraving and Printing Litho.

DEPT. OF TRANSP. U. S. COAST GUARD, CG-2849 (REV 8-67)

# My Sailing Career

*I* *was the oldest of 11 kids growing up in the St. Ignace/* Moran area, and at that time there were many boats in the Straits of Mackinac area. Among them were fishing tugs, island passenger boats, McGregor's Chris Crafts, state ferries and railroad ferries, most of them burning coal. So I developed an interest in boats early on.

I used to see those officers with their uniforms, and I'd tell myself that someday I'd have a uniform and my own boat. It was only a dream, but it became a reality.

I got through school in 1935 and worked on the Michigan State Ferries for three years. Desiring a mate's license, I quit and went on the ore freighters, since you could only get a license for the waters you worked on, and I didn't want a license that was good only for the Straits area.

I was always big for my age. Dad had a farm, so I learned early how to work, and never had trouble finding a job. As a junior in high school, I was caring for the lawn of the Colonial House in the middle of town, right near the State Ferry dock. Pat Rhodes, a state foreman, asked me if I'd care to work as a temporary relief on the ferry St. Ignace, which was due in about a half hour. He told me to run home and get a change of clothes.

I told him I was ready; I had my change of clothes on. That was in 1934.

The winter of 1942–43 I went to marine navigation school in Port Huron and secured my pilot's license. Glenn Shaw of DeTour and I had gone down together for the six-week course. We both passed the Coast Guard test with scores in the upper 90 percentile.

After three days of writing the Coast Guard exam I knew I was going to make it, so I wrote six letters for 3rd mate jobs. I wanted the companies to get my letters before they were swamped with other 3rd mate applications. This initiative paid off, as I got five job promises. I was more eager to get on with a secure company than I was about promotion, because I had two young boys to raise; so I chose the International Harvester Company. After five years, realizing I had made a mistake, I quit. On the advice of my captain I took a captain's job on the excursion ship Wayne, which was an auto ferry from Detroit to Windsor at that time.

I knew it wasn't going to be a job with a future, but I would gain boat-handling experience and become more familiar with the Coast Guard. I believe I made the right choice, as I did get a lot of experience. I quit in the fall to go on the ore carriers and to be lined up for a spring job.

Because of my limited income that season, I went to work as a relief mate on the Ann Arbor car ferries during the winter months. That was a job I worked on every winter after that from 1947 to 1982, when they folded. The last two years I worked mostly as 1st mate and captain. They always had a job for me when I needed work, so I never refused when they needed me. I liked working on the car ferries.

The steamer E. G. Grace and my ship once locked through the Sault Locks together en route to Duluth. Weather was westerly about 20 miles per hour—overcast, steady glass, but with an odd look in the air. The Grace was faster and passed me. Our weather report was good, so when we got to Whitefish Point the Grace rounded the point and steered on for Duluth. I felt uncomfortable about it, but didn't know why. Along my way I had never allowed other boats to decide what I was going to do.

If the Grace hadn't been there, I probably wouldn't have hesitated, but I decided to steer northeast and up the eastern shore of

Lake Superior. Then, if the wind did go northwesterly, I'd be in the lee of the north shore and would have good going.

About six hours later, out of the blue, the wind switched to a northwesterly gale force. I guess it was a sixth sense on my part; however, things went well for us. But in talking to the captain of the Grace a couple of days later, I found out he had checked her down and had bucked heavy seas for two days.

Incidentally, we beat the Grace to Duluth.

Often along the way, you do something without a reason. You don't know why, but it turns out to be the right choice.

During my sailing days there were many small lumber hookers, tugs and tows, tugs and lumber rafts, many 450 feet or longer—steamboats towing ore barges near the same size, many tankers and passenger boats. All bulk boats and self-unloaders had their pilot houses forward and the booms placed forward.

Today the modern boats have all cabins and unloading booms aft. There are just a couple of tankers left, no passenger vessels and only a few tugs and barges still around.

For a while I sold made-to-measure suits on the boat. A huge watchman wanted a suit. He was about six-foot-two and weighed about 400 pounds. His neck was about a 22, his thighs and stomach really large. He was somewhat stooped and had an "apron belly," meaning that his belly hung below his crotch. So I got some graph paper and drew him to scale, with a measurement about every 10 inches, showing how far below his crotch his belly hung. Then I picked out a navy hard-finish suit with a stripe and three pairs of pants.

I sent the order in and received a call asking if I was sure the measurements were correct. I told them, "Yes, make it up." The suit came and I couldn't have been more pleased . It fit him perfectly. After that, I sold nearly everyone on the boat a suit. The watchman was so pleased, he gave me an extra $20.

I docked the steamer Ben Morrel in Duluth and the International was at the dock next to me. I went over to visit my former captain, but the mate told me he was shopping in Duluth, and that the Pathfinder was due at his spot in a half hour, so they were going to finish loading the International at the next dock. He said they were looking for the captain, but would I mind shifting the International, since I knew the captain well.

I told the mate I would do it. Since the engine was all warmed up, I shifted her in about a half hour, and the Pathfinder followed me right in. Normally that's not the thing to do, but as it turned out in this case it was in everyone's favor. When the captain returned, he and I had coffee together and all was well.

One captain on the W. C. Richardson was a heavy drinker. One day, while going down the Saginaw River, the watchman on the bow yelled up to him, "How much longer to the dock, Captain?" and he answered, "Oh, about six cans of beer."

Once when he went back for his dinner, I had the watchman use a razor blade and shave the end of a manila rope until we had a small glass full of manila shavings. Then we sprinkled the shavings on the captain's bed sheets.

The next day as we went down the river, the captain was scratching to relieve the itching. We told him, "We're itchy, too, Captain."

Years ago they used to tow a large raft of logs behind a tug from Canada to American paper plants, such as from Marathon, Ontario, to Ashland, WI. A small assist tug followed, in case the logs' outer circle retaining boom broke open. The small tug would gather up the scattered logs, return them to the barrier and again secure the log boom.

One night in dense fog, a small Steel Trust freighter with water ballast pumped out, so only her propeller was well submerged, heard the tug's fog signal and steered to clear the tug. The tug towing the log raft had about a 300-foot tow line, and about an 800-foot by

300-foot raft of logs.

The freighter cleared the tug, but skipped right into the raft of logs. So he called the tug on his radio phone, and asked that he part his boom of logs, so he could get going. The tug skipper told him, "Stay there until daylight, and we'll free you." So the tug towed his raft of logs and his boat company all night, and freed them in the morning.

Back when I shipped watchman on the 600-foot ore freighter Augustus B. Wolvin (launched in 1904) my watch was 2 to 6 p.m. and a.m. One-half hour before the end of my watch, my job was to clean the pilot house for the next watch. Included in my cleanup duties was taking the filthy gaboon, a "catch-all," set on the deck in front of the wheelsman to catch cigarette butts, cigar butts, tobacco juice and spit. I did this for about a month. I never smoked or chewed tobacco. One morning I cleaned up, but never touched the gaboon.

Going out the door with my bucket and mop, I heard the mate say, "Hold it, Mac; haven't you forgotten something?" So I looked around and purposely missed the gaboon. "No, I don't think so, Mate. I got everything." He said, "You missed the gaboon." I said, "Yes, I did —on purpose. I've never smoked or chewed, and that filthy gaboon sickens me. He said, "You'll clean it, or get off when we get to Ashtabula." I said, "Okay, I'll get off."

About five hours before Ashtabula, the captain called me to his office. I thought, "Cripes, what now?" The captain, a nice, older man, said, "McGrath, I understand you're getting off." I said, "Yes, Sir. I never smoked, and that gaboon sickens me." He said, "What if I change the rules, buy three new brass gaboons, and each wheelsman brings his own clean gaboon on watch and takes it down with him at the end of his watch and cleans it." I said, "Okay, Captain. Thank you. I'll stay."

Three weeks later, I was promoted to wheelsman, on the mate's watch, and he made darn sure that my gaboon was really filthy at the end of my watch. He both chewed and smoked, so that gaboon was busy my four hours on watch. I couldn't complain; because of me, the rule had been changed.

I stayed on that boat and wheeled for the next two years.

In the 70s on the Kinsman Independent, we had a load of grain for the Standard Elevator in Buffalo. We got loaded about 2 a.m., so we departed up to the turning basin to wind (turn) on down through two bridges and to the break wall light.

About 4:30 a.m. I lay down, and got up for breakfast about 7:30. I walked into the dining room, and there was a young couple, about 17 years of age, sitting there. I asked, "What are you guys doing here?" The girl said, "We always wanted a boat ride, and knew we'd never get one. So when everyone was busy, we sneaked aboard and hid in a lifeboat."

I told them my name and asked the 2nd cook to take their order. They were really hungry. Both had double orders. I brought them forward and gave them the guest room, then took them to the pilothouse and asked the wheelsman to teach them how to steer. Later I asked the mate to have someone escort them all around the boat.

We got to Detroit about 6 a.m. the next day. I called Nicholson's dock and asked if I could tie up for about 10 minutes. I gave each of the kids $20 for bus fare back to Buffalo.

About two months later, I got a thank-you card, my $40, and word that they were engaged. About three years later, I received a card announcing the arrival of a baby boy. His name was Bobby Ray— Bobby after the father and Ray after me. I sent them a gift check.

The father, Bobby, got a steady job as an elevator repair man, so they were doing OK, and I was pleased. Come to think of it, that kid is grown up—that was 1973!

While working on the state ferries, my friend Fred ran out of white paint while painting his kitchen. Going through the ship's paint locker he found a couple of quarts and, at the day's end, he took the paint and was walking up the dock. The mate met him and asked,

"What do you have there, Fred?" Fred said, "About two quarts of paint that I need." Mate said, "Take 30 days off without pay."

About a month later that mate was going home and in front of the state ferry office, as the marine superintendent was coming out of the office, the mate's bag fell apart and steaks, fruit and cans of food fell to the sidewalk. The shore captain said, "Mate, take 30 days off without pay." I couldn't have been more pleased.

Once I was captain on a grain freighter, and about an hour before we were to be unloaded, a young couple knocked on my door and asked if I could marry them aboard the boat. I told them I could, but they'd have to get it legalized later. However, if they still wanted me to "mock-marry" them, and take pictures, I would. They decided against it, and I was glad; I didn't want that new business. That was years ago, during sailing ship days; on-ship marriages were often done because of long voyages.

Once as we were coming out of port, the watchman was rinsing off the deck in front of the pilot house. Not thinking what he was doing as he turned around, he squirted water right in the front window and got the captain, who had had a little too much to drink. The captain blew for me and said, "The seas are coming right over the bow. Break out the whole crew and get those tarps on." We had a wind about 10 miles per hour and the lake looked like a millpond.

Another time, we were going down the Detroit River in heavy fog and the radar broke down just as we entered the Livingstone Cut, which is like a big ditch 300 feet wide and of solid rock. So the 3rd mate and I each got a five-gallon pail filled with baseball-sized lumps of coal and went in front of the pilot house. Every three minutes I'd throw a piece of coal to the right, and he'd throw one to the left. If they splashed in the water, we knew we were okay. If we heard the coal hit rock, we knew we were getting too close to the bank on that side. We were practically through that three-mile cut before the weather finally cleared up.

I was 1st mate once when my captain knew that the cook was stealing, but couldn't catch him in the act. The cook would order groceries or linen, and have part of the order delivered to his own house. So the captain got company stationery and wrote a letter about our thieving cook, using carbon paper to produce a copy of the letter. Then he threw the original away and put a blank sheet of paper in the envelope, stamped and sealed it. He laid the envelope on his desk on top of the carbon copy. He then went aft for his dinner, knowing the cook would be coming in to make up his room, and would probably read the carbon letter and believe the original was in that envelope.

When we got back next trip, the company personnel man and company lawyer met us with the letter the cook sent to the company, knocking the captain. The captain denied writing a letter, saying that he had always treated the cook well. The personnel man fired the cook and our problem was solved.

I was going ashore in Buffalo just as a young sailor was returning to the ship, and he said, "I just made a fast thirteen bucks." I asked how and he said that an elderly lady with a cane had fallen and couldn't get up, so he had helped her and she gave him money, thanked him and said that was all the money she had. So I asked him which way she had gone, and he pointed her out in the next block. I told him, "Come with me." We caught up to her and I gave her back her money, telling her Johnny was sorry he had taken her money. She thanked me. Then I told Johnny to mark down two hours overtime.

I was going over the 106th Street Bridge in South Chicago when I noticed a freighter approaching, so I ran and got over the bridge before it opened. When the boat blew for the bridge, a taxicab carrying a female passenger was roaring along, trying to get across the bridge before it opened for the freighter. By the time the cab got to the middle of the bridge, it was already opened about 35 feet. The cab driver flew the span, making a perfect landing on the other side.

The only damage done was to the Radio Cab light on top of

the vehicle. Then he crashed into a guard rail, and called to another cab, who came and got the passenger. I asked the dock boss to save me the next few *Chicago Tribunes*, but the incident never made the papers.

Getting back to my drinking captain: It was the middle of August, and really hot (about 95°). We were going into Marblehead Stone dock, near Sandusky, OH. I was on deck preparing to dock the vessel when the wheelsman, named David, came down on deck and said, "I think the captain's passed out in the pilot house." I checked, and sure enough, he was passed out in the large chair. All around the pilot house were large quarter-inch glass windows and doors. So I closed all the windows and doors and went down to load the boat.

About two hours later, the captain showed up on deck wringing wet from sweat. The gang got a kick out of that.

Once I was coming down the eastern shore of Lake Huron in a 35-mile-per-hour wind out of the east. The mate sighted a small boat with a white cloth waving, so we went over to check on him. It was a 12-foot canoe carrying a man and his 12-year-old daughter; they had been fishing near the Canadian shore when the wind picked up and they were unable to handle the canoe. They were being blown across the lake toward the Michigan shore, and it was getting late in the afternoon, and cold.

We got on the windward side of them and threw them a couple of lines, which they secured on both ends of the canoe. Then we lowered a landing chair on the end of a 10-foot boom and hoisted them up, the girl first. The father was really pleased and wanted no more to do with his canoe. He offered to sell it to me. I told him I had no use for it, but if he wanted to trust me I'd give him $100 and half of whatever I could sell it for. He said that was fine and we had a deal.

It took me five years before I found a good buyer who gave me $600 for the canoe. I sent the man $300 and figured I came out about $100 ahead on the deal. I heard from him for quite a while after that, and did hear that his daughter was going to college to be a lawyer.

While living in Chicago, I used to play poker twice a week at a neighborhood bar. One night the bartender said, "I have some stew left over from supper. Would any of you care for a bowl?" I said, "I would." It was good, so later on I got a second bowl. At the end of the game when I was getting ready to leave, the bartender asked, "Do you know what kind of stew that was? Muskrat." Had I known that, I might have turned it down, but it was good. I understand a muskrat washes everything before it eats it.

We had a large water glass on our card table, and anytime the pot was over $5 we'd put a quarter in the glass, and when the bartender brought beer over he'd take the money out of the glass. At the end of the night we'd leave the glass for the bartender's tip. However, the night cop on duty would occasionally come in, get a shot and a beer, and a couple of cigars, and then dump our glass of quarters in his side pocket and take off, paying for nothing.

We had a watchman who was six-foot-eleven, and the tendons controlling his toes were shrinking, which made his toes curl under like a bird's claws. He wore a wide tennis shoe so his toes had plenty of room.

One winter he went to the hospital and had his foot problem corrected. The nurse who cared for him was extremely nice to him; he wound up marrying her, and they lived in International Falls, MN near the Canadian border.

Along my way I had one especially talented 1st mate, Robert Zeitler. He was an all-around excellent mate. On top of that, he kept our radar and gyro going. We seldom had to call for a service man. He surely was a great help to me; I will always remember him.

One time on a railroad car ferry we were en route to the Sturgeon Bay Canal in a blinding snowstorm. I took a radio direction finder bearing on the light and found it to be about 30° on the right, so told the captain. He also took a bearing and said, "It's on the left, where it should be." A few minutes later I told the captain, "That breakwall light is now about 40° on our right. He said, "You Great Lakes mates are all the same." Just then the snow let up a bit and there was the flashing red light, 45° on our right. The captain told the wheelsman to make a hard left. We had to make a complete circle to come into the entrance with that breakwall on our left. He never criticized my bearings readings again . . . but made no apologies, either.

The Steel Vendor, a crane boat with a cargo of scrap iron, was downbound off Copper Harbor in a strong northwesterly gale when she suddenly took a prominent list. They figured they were going to lose her, but she limped on down to Chicago.

A good friend of mine was on her. Figuring she was going to go down, and being close to Copper Harbor, he dived off to swim ashore before she got too far down the lake. He was the only one who got lost. He never made it.

I was eastbound at the Straits and met a westbound German salt water tanker. I asked him, "What do you have for cargo?" He said, "We have a full cargo of horse urine, bound for Milwaukee. Its principle use is for tanning hides, and it has other uses as well." I didn't believe him. So later I called another salt water tanker and he said, "That's right. Occasionally we do carry that."

The crew aboard a lake freighter, when I was sailing, consisted of a captain; 1st, 2nd and 3rd mates; three wheelsmen; three watchmen; and three deckhands.

The galley consisted of a chief cook, 2nd cook and two porters.

The engineer's crew consisted of a chief engineer; 1st, 2nd and 3rd assistant engineers; three oilers; three firemen; and three coal passers.

This is a total of 30 persons on board. If you happen to be on a self-unloader, with a 250-foot self-unloading boom, you usually had four more men for a total of 34.

The captain and chief engineer were on call 24 hours a day. All others were assigned four-hour watches: 1st mate and 1st engineer—4–8 a.m. & p.m.; 2nd mate and 2nd engineer—12–4 a.m. & p.m.; 3rds' watch—8–12 a.m. & p.m. The galley crew was split, with hours off between meals. But the 2nd cook was the baker and got up about 4:30 a.m. to do his baking. Today it's mostly store-bought baked goods.

Young deckhands were assigned watches, but were kept on days to keep the ship maintained—scrubbing, chipping and painting.

The watchmen worked their watches and maintained the boat, running the steam winches in docking and in leaving docks; loading and unloading; dropping the anchor; opening and closing the steel hatches.

The wheelsman worked his watch, ran deck winches and steered the boat. Often you hear wheelsmen talking about how they know the rivers, or how they round the curves, or how difficult it is to steer in the fog. This is all myth. Each wheelsman has a mate who's the pilot in the wheelhouse. He has a Coast Guard's certified pilot's license. And it's he, the mate, who's running the rivers and the show. He tells the wheelsman when to start turning; and if it's not coming just right, he will tell the wheelsman to come more quickly or more slowly.

The wheelsman steers by gyro, which is an electrically-operated compass with the direction in numeral degrees from 0° to 360°. Each degree sounds a click. So the mate tells the wheelsman, "Steer course 75°." So that's all he has to do, keep her on 75°. However, today with automatic steering, in the open lake you just set your course and drink coffee.

In today's modern vessels, with satellite navigation equipment, you can program your courses, say, from Whitefish to Duluth, which normally has about five course changes, and the vessel will run each course and haul automatically. If a side wind picks up, it'll haul a degree or two into the wind to make your programmed course correct. But I never sailed on those jobs.

All the boats I sailed on had their pilot houses forward, or on the stem, and their engineers' quarters aft, or on the stern. Today, with all quarters aft, living together, the crews should get along better. When I sailed there was always a little friction. We used to refer to the engineer's crew as nut-busters, or Black Gang—probably because most boats burned coal.

When I first started to sail in 1935, many of the boats did not have gyro-compasses; most had magnetic compasses. Many did not have radio telephones, but operated with the telegraph. Many still had wooden hatches, and we had to remove them by hand. We had radio direction finders—an electric radio pointer system in which each port had a different signal. For instance, Ludington was 4 longs (— — — —), Milwaukee was 2 longs (— —), others could be a combination of longs and shorts. Each would broadcast at a certain time period, maybe four times an hour.

When Milwaukee's signal came on, the signals were really loud; but as you swung your pointer closer to Milwaukee's direction, it would get weaker. When you were exactly at Milwaukee's port, the signal would cut out completely and there was silence. So we took that degree bearing, and then take, say, Racine's bearing, and plot those two courses on the chart. Where they'd cross would be your exact position. With radar today, along with the Loran System, that old method is seldom used.

Also, very few ships were equipped with radar. Before the Coast Guard controlled the rivers, I often entered the rivers at DeTour, passed through the Locks and on up to Whitefish, and never saw another ship except at the Locks. I've entered and departed many, many ports with hardly any visibility—say, 50 feet maximum. On a calm day, with radar, you can pick up a beer can on your screen. It's the interpretation of what's on the radar screen that makes it important and useful.

Also, in my early days on the ships, most boats had no refrigeration. We'd carry ice aboard each time we'd get groceries.

We had no depthometers to find the depth of the water. When going to anchor, we had a "lead line"—a long half-inch line with about a 16-pound deep-sea lead on one end. This lead was about 12–15 inches long, about 3½ inches wide at one end, and about 3 inches wide with a ring on the small end. The larger end had a hole about 2 inches in diameter drilled in the bottom of the lead weight, and rope marked every six feet. We'd jam mild soap or pliable wax in this hole so when we read the wet portion of the line, we'd know the depth of the water, and by looking at the end we'd know whether the bottom was sand, gravel or mud.

Most boats were hand coal-fired boilers, and all the firemen crabbed about bad coal. Never once did I hear a fireman say we had really good fuel.

I had a refrigerator, hot plate and coffee pot in my quarters, so didn't always go back for meals. I also had a TV, radio and cribbage board, so I was pretty well set.

We were loading grain in Duluth for Buffalo and were almost finished when a young wheelsman knocked on my office door. He had called home and his girlfriend had just gone into the hospital to have a baby. He wanted to get off for four days, and then catch us in Buffalo. We had no time to replace him. I gave him a draw and told him to get going. He was on the 8 to 12 watches, so the mate did the steering and I stood the mate's watch. I kept the wheelsman's salary going and paid the mate overtime. Everything turned out okay. I figured that if he thought that much of his girl, he was an O.K. guy. He was pleased. They were married that winter.

Once I had a drinking captain who claimed that the only kind of liquor he could drink was Seagram's VO. So I had the watchman sneak into his room and empty his VO bottle, refilling it with "Snug-Harbor," a cheap rotgut whiskey. He drank her down and never complained.

My room was next to his quarters, with thin walls. He'd go on a drinking spree for about four or five days, then straighten up, shower, shave, and pray. I could hear him praying, often for half an hour at a time; then he'd come up to the pilot house all cleaned up, and complain about the drunks aboard, telling me to get rid of them.

Occasionally he'd have one of the crew pass the hat for a collection "for the poor people in Hungary," then claim he took it to the church. I very much doubt if the church ever saw him or his collection. Those who didn't want to give, he'd give them a couple hours of overtime. So, they'd give.

Needless to say, I respected his position—but surely not him.

Warren Highstone, a St. Ignace businessman wintering in Fort Lauderdale, FL, and a strong supporter of the New York Yankees, used up all of his contacts and couldn't get tickets to a weekend Yankees game. While driving around he noticed an office with a sign that said "New York Yankees Winter Office," so he went in and said, "I don't know George Steinbrenner, but I know his captain, Ray I. McGrath. On the strength of that, could I get tickets for the Yankees game?"

They told him, "George is not here now, but leave your phone number." Later Steinbrenner called him and asked how many were in his party. Warren said six. George said, "Pick up your tickets at the office."

When Warren opened the envelope he found eight tickets to the game. When he and his party got to the game they found that their tickets were Steinbrenner's box seats, and when Mr. Steinbrenner passed him he introduced himself. That really made Warren's day. Sometime later I received a letter from Warren saying that he hoped

I hadn't minded his using my name, but that he just had to get some tickets. I was amused by his method. Later he sent me a couple of Yankee baseball caps.

You don't hear much about the positive things George Steinbrenner does, but years ago he started a college program. He picked 20 kids who were poverty-stricken, all-A students, and paid all of their tuition, room and board, books, clothes—everything for their seven-year terms, all studying to be lawyers or doctors. When they graduated, they had to pay back with no interest. If one reneged and didn't repay him, he would only carry 19 students the next year. In 25 years he never lost a student.

In 1974, Steinbrenner had around 25 boats in his fleet and he was still president of American Shipbuilding Company. Many of the boats had names that didn't mean anything to Steinbrenner.

Ted Kennedy was running for office again, so I wrote him a note and suggested that if he had George put his name on one of the boats, every time one of the boats would call "Steamer Senator Ted Kennedy" he'd be getting free advertising.

Kennedy sent me a handwritten note thanking me for my interest in him, but said that in no way would he ever want to be obligated to George Steinbrenner.

To show how our Great Lakes steamboat business has dwindled in the last 37 years —In 1956, the following companies were active:
√ Steel Trust—60 boats and 3 tugs
√ Interlake—32 boats
√ Cleveland Cliffs—17 boats
√ Columbia—17 boats
√ Great Lakes Steamship Co.—16 boats
√ Hutchinson—17 boats
Today (1996) the total number of American boats is about 55.

Three mates I had who are now captains and know I have a

scanner, occasionally blow me a salute: one long and two short blasts on the whistle, which says "hello" in sailor language. And once in a while they will radio-phone a "hello," like: "Hi, Captain Ray I." I really appreciate that.

Long before my time, on the lakes there was always a taboo about starting a sailing season on a Friday. If you were all ready to go on a Friday, you waited until a couple of minutes after midnight before taking off.

One spring the Coast Guard inspectors gave me my certificate about 9 a.m. Friday; I thanked them, trotted up to a telephone, called the office, and told them. They said, "Fine, plan on leaving a few minutes after midnight." It was a Friday the 13th, and I told them, "If you don't mind, I'd like to leave now." They said, "Fine; you're the captain—go." So I took off. The gang was not too happy, but we were on our way. It turned out to be one of my better seasons.

When I got my pilot's license, the captains used to run the rivers in clear or dense fog with a stop watch, with the boat light or loaded. He always recorded the time lapse, so that in fog he'd run the time and haul. Surprisingly we had few mishaps. Now they have extremely sensitive radar, and it is "on" all the time. Come river time the Coast Guard orders them to anchor—which, of course, is far safer. But we have to give the old-time captains credit; they did an excellent job.

I was once downbound between Whitefish and Gros Cap lights when I noticed a lady frantically waving a red cloth or sweater, yelling that her motor boat engine was dead. We tossed her a line and life belt, and she came up the ladder. We had a deckhand who volunteered to ride in the motor boat. We gave him about 300 feet of light line to use as a tow line, and proceeded to the Sault at slow speed. After about a half hour he got the motor boat engine running, tossed off our line, passed us and took off for the Sault. We tied up at the

MacArthur Lock and lowered our ladder; the woman went down to her boat and the deckhand came aboard.

She sent a letter to our company thanking them, and they forwarded the letter to us. We were pleased to be able to help her.

I was 1st mate on the Ruth Webster when, an hour out of Buffalo, I called the captain and he was so sick, he couldn't get out of bed. He asked me to take her in on the "Q.T." I did and never told anyone. The following day he went to the doctor and was pronounced okay.

We never mentioned the incident.

Before unions, if you had a promising, sharp, hard worker, you could sort of take an interest in him, teach and promote him along. Now, if a kid is watching and would like a wheelsman job, he can't accept a wheelsman berth on his ship. The union says he must quit, go up to the union hall and sign up for a wheelsman job, and then wait his turn. In the meantime, his boat may wind up with someone who can't really wheel and is undesirable. But that's the way she goes.

I am sure the shore-side public seldom gives a thought to our life aboard ship:

We are all on work watches, day and night. The captain and chief are on call anytime. The cook's department only works days, and their hours are arranged to cover the three meals.

During stormy weather, the cooks wet down the tablecloths so the dishes won't slide, and in really bad weather they put rolling bars on the tables so the dishes can't slide off the tables. They usually use about half-inch pipe, or smaller, round the table's edges. When boats were smaller, say, up to 500 feet, we always had the lifeline cable stretched 8-10 feet above the deck, with rings and one-inch line attached to the rings. These lines are used by the sailors to steady themselves while going or coming from aft.

Years ago all boats were equipped with barrels of storm oil. In case of salvaging a boat or lowering lifeboats, this storm oil was spread on the water. It wouldn't lessen the seas, but more or less smoothed the sea, and did away with the splashing and foam.

Between watches the sailors read, listen to radio, watch TV, write letters, do their laundry or play cards—poker and cribbage being the favorite games. As a rule, two games of poker are going on, with a 10-cent limit for the young kids and 50 cents for the older guys. On my ship I had a standing rule: they couldn't play within two hours of the beginning of their watch time. Otherwise they'd be sleeping on watch. As a rule, sailors are poor swimmers and treaders.

Should you want to sail, you must first contact a steamship company, or the union, and get a letter promising you a job upon receipt of your seaman card, which is issued by the Coast Guard. After you are screened, you then sail for 18 months and study the rules and regulations ... how to tie knots and splice, how to box the compass, first aid, steering and rowing. With proof of your time, you can then sit for a Coast Guard exam for your "ABs" (Able-Bodied Seaman's Certificate), which entitles you to promotion to watchman and wheelsman.

After another 18 months, you can write for pilot's or mate's license, upon the waters you sailed. This mate's license entitles you to work up to 1st mate; after one year in that position you may write for your Master's license (captain). Then every five years, you must get your radio, radar and license renewed. You can study for renewal on your own, but most go to a marine school because it's tough & new rules come out occasionally.

As a rule of thumb, you normally work about 10 years before being considered for a captain's job. I retired in 1985, renewed my license once, and it is up for renewal again in 1995 —but I'll let it lapse. My license is for all tons on the Great Lakes, and reads: "Master and 1st class Pilot between Duluth, Gary, Buffalo, North Tonawanda and Ogdensburg, New York." Ogdensburg is 65 miles down the St. Lawrence River.

For years the only jobs for a woman were in the galley. Today we have women mates, engineers, captains and chief engineers. Most all of them attend maritime schools and graduate with their licenses, so they step aboard as mates or engineers or stewards. With the seamen's unions today, you work 60 days and are off 30 with pay.

The ship's bell clock is programmed to strike the time in four-hour intervals: two dings for the hour and one ding for the half hour. So the beginning of each watch, or at the end of the first half hour, the clock strikes one bell, for 4:30, 8:30 and 12:30, then 2 bells for 1, 5 and 9 o'clock. For 6:30, 10:30 and 2:30 it would be ding ding, ding ding, & ding—and so forth. 4, 8 and 12 o'clock would be 8 bells. Then the cycle would start again.

The wheelsman then would repeat the time by striking the 10 x 12-inch brass bell fastened to the top of the pilot house, with a rope fastened to the bell's clapper. This bell time can usually be heard all over the boat, and most of the crew are waiting for 8 bells, or the end of their watches.

The bell is also used while the ship is anchored in dense fog, accompanied by the ship's main whistle, upon the approach of another vessel — but is sounded separately.

About 10 minutes before all meals, the porter used to sound an 8 x 4-inch bell with a wooden handle while walking around the after cabin. Today, with most of the boats, there is only one set of cabins aft and no walking-around space, so this practice, like the forward cabins, is long gone.

Normally a short salute (___ - -, or one long blast and two short blasts) on the ship's main stack whistle, is the signal ships blow when meeting a vessel they know, like a "hello." A full salute on the stack whistle is ___ ___ ___ - -, three long blasts followed by two short blasts. Each blast is about two seconds apart, and the meeting ship answers the same. A full salute is not blown often, but you'll often hear ___ - -, the shorter salute.

When a ship enters the lock or a dock, and comes to the tie-up spot, they blow two short blasts, which means "tie up." When ready to leave, they blow one short blast, and the dock handlers will throw their lines off.

When two ships are meeting and wish to pass to the right of each other, one ship blows one long blast and the answering vessel will give a long blast. If they want to meet to the left of each other, they'll blow two long blasts. If the vessel hearing the one long blast, signifying a wish to pass to the right, wishes to meet on the left instead, she'll answer with five or more short blasts, which is the danger signal, and follow with two long blasts, signifying she wants to pass to the left. The answering vessel will acknowledge with two long blasts.

Another use of the main stack whistle: when using a tug, the signals are relayed thus —one blast, "go ahead"; one blast, "stop"; two blasts will always mean "back up", regardless of previously-given signals; three blasts, "check" or "ease up"; four blasts mean "really strong"; and usually a long and short mean "O.K., finished with tug."

Approaching the Sault Locks, about a half mile away either up or down river, we'd blow a long blast on the whistle, signifying we wanted a lock. The lockmaster would give us a lock with a light signaling set-up. One light signifies MacArthur Lock; two lights, Poe Lock; and three lights on board meant to take the third lock. We would then acknowledge that we had received the lock signal by answering with a long and short blast. Today we use a radio telephone.

The Coast Guard Marine Inspection checks your vessel and its equipment, to make sure all is in working order before making your first trip. Occasionally they will make an unscheduled visit and hold a fire and boat drill, and quickly check your operating gear to make sure all is in working order.

The Pittsburgh Supply warehouse, about a mile east of the Locks, has a supply vessel, the Ojibway, equipped with a hoisting crane that brings supplies, such as groceries, engine and deck supplies. If personnel are changing, they bring them out to the freighters. No one is allowed to board or depart the vessels in the Lock for security reasons.

Entering the lock, one deck officer takes the outgoing mail to the marine post office and returns with the incoming mail.

Both forward and after end draft marks are read by the U. S. Corps of Engineers on all vessels entering the Locks. Each boat can load only so deep. The penalty fine used to be $1,000 for each inch that you were over your specified draft marks.

Every five years, all boats go into the shipyard for a total Coast Guard inspection. They check all plates, rivets, wheel, rudder, and all working gear. They then issue a certificate that is good for five years. No vessel can sail without this inspection certificate.

A round-trip from Duluth to Buffalo to Duluth, was about 10 days, so I'd take my wife, Lou, on a two- or three-week trip ride. She'd get off, mow the grass, and be back for another ride.

My wife made trips with me on all the lake freighters and car ferries when I worked on as captain, and on some I worked on as mate. Over all, she rode on perhaps 30 different boats. Her grandfather and father were both chief engineers.

As 1st mate, I often took the boat in and out of ports in nice weather. Finished loading coal at South Chicago, I told the watch man to tell the captain we were loaded and ready to go. He came back and said, "He's sleeping." So I took her out, en route to Muskegon. I didn't know until the next day that we had left the captain. He waited until we were about one quarter unloaded before coming aboard in Muskegon. All turned out O.K. — but after that time, I checked personally.

I was lucky. I never had an accident or a grounding, but I did get caught in a few bad storms.

The captain on the Fred R. White, Captain Ed Drummond, was once my deckhand. I promoted him to temporary watchman until he got his A. B. ticket (A. B.—Able-Bodied Seaman, meaning you had passed the Coast Guard test). I told him that upon getting his A. B. ticket, the job was his. After he earned the ticket, I told him that upon learning to splice wire cable, he could have the next wheelsman's job.

About a month later he rapped on my office door one night and said, "Captain, I can splice now." I told him, "Good. The next wheelsman's job is yours."

Ed climbed the ladder and became captain not too many years ago. While passing through St. Ignace he called me to join him for a cup of coffee. While visiting, he said, "Captain, I have a confession to make. I never did learn to splice cable."

I wheeled for a strict but fair mate on the Robert Hobson. One morning, coming off watch, he said to me, "Drop down to my room for a minute." So I did, and he handed me a loading book, about 4 inches by 7 inches, and said, "All the boats I've loaded are in this book in detail for various cargoes and drafts. I have gotten word I am to be the next captain, so I really won't need this any longer. It's also got the number of gallons of paint needed to paint different sized boats, and most information a 1st mate needs. Take good care of it, and when your turn comes as mate, you'll have more help than I had." I thanked him and had the book bound in light leather.

Although commercial freighters and large passenger boats no longer visit St. Ignace (where Lou and I make our home) it is still a very active marine port, with three ferry lines running between St. Ignace, Mackinac Island and Mackinaw City, and many small craft and cruisers. The Straits area is very active. Cedarville, too, has more than its share of pleasure boats, and many islands. That area is just beautiful.

Once I picked up Paul LaMarre and his wife Leeanne in Detroit for a trip up the lake. Paul's a marine artist. Upon our arrival in Duluth a deckhand quit and I couldn't get a replacement, so I wrote a letter to the Coast Guard for Leeanne to get her Seaman's document. She got it, and was on deck with the gang painting on the way down the lake. She really enjoyed it.

That was an exception, as the only woman working on boats at that time was in the galley, usually a man/wife cook combination. However, now there are quite a few lady officers, and I understand Patterson Co. of Canada has a lady captain on a large lake freighter.

While I was mate on the steamship W. W. Holloway, we had a cargo of wheat for winter storage at a grain elevator in Chicago. To fulfill insurance company rules, which said that someone had to be on the ship all winter while it was laid up, my wife and I kept ship, and I was in charge of the unloading gang. The gang didn't have to be sailors, but usually were. So I got a crew of 12 men together, and in the course of 10 or 11 days we unloaded her and shifted to another dock so that another ship could unload. We unloaded storage grain for a couple of months.

About two years later, Lou and I were in a restaurant and I thought I recognized the waitress. Just before we left, I told her, "It seems I know you, but don't know how," and she said, "You're Captain McGrath and I worked for you for two months unloading grain boats. Remember, I always wore a black wool "chuke" with the initials ABC on the front, and heavy clothes. I never took my hat off."

Then I remembered—her name was A. B. Collins, and no one ever knew she was a female. She had run an electric winch for me and was a good worker. It was nice to see her again.

When I worked, I got on a boat April 1st and off about December 15th. In my 50 years of sailing, 1935-85, I got off twice for three days at a time, when my mother-in-law died and when my father died. I worked on the Lake Michigan car ferries during the winter months, so really, I never knew my two sons as they were growing up.

I went captain in 1963 and retired in 1985. I was captain on a

80

total of 23 boats, including the Ann Arbor car ferries.

After 50 years of sailing, I don't miss the boats at all. Most boats I worked on were 600-footers and shorter. Every time a new thousand-footer was built, about six 600-footers were scrapped. Now the only existing boat that I worked on is the 620-foot Joseph H. Frantz. It seems like it was only a few years ago that she was their largest flagship. Often I'll remember some of the sailors who did me favors.

After making the dock in a heavy downpour, the six-foot-four captain came down on deck and looked down at the five-foot-two watchman and said, "Johnny, do you think it'll ever stop raining?" Little Johnny looked up and said, "If it don't, Captain, it'll be a damned long rain."

W.W. Holloway - 1906

# *My Boats*

*The Viking ~ see p.186*

**1935**    Michigan State Ferry St. Ignace, 165 x 45 x 14; carried 35 autos and 415 passengers. This was my first sailing job. She ran the Straits of Mackinac from St. Ignace to Mackinaw City.

**1935**    State Ferry Mackinaw City, 165 x 45 x 14; I worked on her four months, April through July.

**1936**    State Ferry Straits of Mackinac, 196 x 48 x 15; she was the pride of the three-boat fleet and the flag ship. I worked on her for the last 4½ months of 1936.

**1937**    State Ferry City of Cheboygan; she was 250 x 54 x 19 and carried 80 autos and 432 passengers. She was formerly named the Ann Arbor #4 car ferry, out of Frankfort, MI. Her captain was Capt. Andy Coleman. I really liked this ferry.

**1936–38**    I worked winters on the car ferry Sainte Marie, carrying 16 railroad cars and 400 passengers; and on the Chief Wawatam, which was 338.8 x 62 x 25 and carried 26 railroad cars and 516 passengers. I worked the railroad ferries only during the winter months. They had forward engine propellers, which made them more capable of winter navigation.

**1938**    Quit the ferries and got a job on the ore carrier Cygnus, which was 420 x 52 x 28. I thought she was really huge. Her captain, Robert Leach of St. Clair, MI, was 45 years old and this was his first captain's job.

**1938**    After laying up the Cygnus about December 15, the captain asked me if I'd like to make a trip or two on the steamer

Hemlock. So I worked on her for about three weeks. She was the same size as the Cygnus. The thing I most remember about the Hemlock is her captain's beautiful penmanship.

**1939**     Worked the state ferries City of Petoskey and City of Munising, each 338 x 56 x 196. They carried 120 autos and 600 passengers, and I spent approximately four months on each of them. All of the Michigan State Ferries were painted white. In fog or a snow storm, they were extremely hard to see.

**1940–43**     I was appointed watchman on the Robert W. E. Bunsen for the Steel Trust Company. She was fitting out in South Chicago. I reported for work about the middle of April, but the company doctor said I had a rupture, so sent me to the Marine Hospital. After a checkup I was told to go back to my boat, that I did not have a rupture. So the company doctor checked me again and said, "You do have a rupture." So I took my bag and checked in at the Lake Shipping Hall, and soon got a ship, the Augustus B. Wolvin, the first big iron ship and the first 600-foot vessel on the Great Lakes. I shipped on as a watchman, and six weeks later was promoted to wheelsman. I wheeled in 1940–41, studied all the time and wrote for my pilot's license the winter of 1941. I passed my Coast Guard exam, and in the spring of 1942, I went 3rd mate on the International, owned by International Harvester Company. I stayed 3rd mate for 2½ seasons and was promoted to 2nd mate in the middle of the 1943 season.

**1943–45**     During this period I remained 2nd mate.

**1946**     I went 2nd mate on their second boat, the Harvester, and kept ship on her the winter of 1946-47.

**1947**     In the spring of 1947, I went captain on the excursion boat Wayne, which ran across the Detroit River before the bridge was built and now was making excursion runs out of Duluth, three trips a day, about 1½ hours per trip. The owner of the ferry was a shady character, but I agreed to work for $250 less than my $500 monthly wage, so the boat could make more money, and let them pay me a lump sum at the end of the season. However, after getting to know him quite well, I was sure there was no way he was going to pay me the balance of my wage. So I quit working for him the middle of August after securing a job as 3rd mate on Columbia's Wolverine, a 450-foot wooden hatch boat, and a workhorse. We usually carried coal upbound and grain downbound. I was on her only one season as 3rd mate, and we laid up in Buffalo.

Because of a tough summer, I worked on the Frankfort Ann Arbor car ferries during the winter of 1947, and for many winters after that.

**1947–48** '47 was a bad year, so I worked on the Ann Arbor car ferries out of Frankfort, MI during the winter. (In those days we had no unemployment checks.) I worked from Dec. 15, 1947–April 1, 1948 on the Ann Arbor #6 and the Wabash, mostly as 3rd mate.

**1948** Was 3rd mate on the grain carrier Wolverine, a boat with wooden hatches. Worked from April 3 to December 12.

**1948–49** Again was relief mate, mostly 3rd mate, on the car ferries and went where I was needed. Worked until May 1, 1949.

**1949** Late call, went to work May 15 on Columbia's self-unloader the R. E. Moody, and worked on her until October 30. On November 11 I went 3rd mate on the self-unloader E. G. Mathiott, and laid her up in Fairport, OH on Dec. 21.

**1949–50** Was again relief mate on the car ferries until May 10, 1950.

**1950** Went 2nd mate on the Carrollton from May 15 to June 30, then was transferred to the E. G. Mathiott as 2nd mate and laid her up in South Chicago on December 15.

**1951** Went 2nd mate on the E. G. Mathiott March 7 and laid her up in Fairport, OH on December 10.

**1952**     Was 2nd mate again on the E. G. Mathiott from March 10 until May 28, when I went 1st mate until June 24. At that time I was again 2nd mate and laid the E. G. Mathiott up on December 12 in Toledo, OH.

**1953**     Was 1st mate on the steamer William F. Stifel. Capt. Ernest McSorley was her captain , always a gentleman.

**1954**     Was 1st mate on the E. G. Mathiott from April 4 until May 22, then transferred to the steamer Carrollton and was 1st mate until layup on December 16 in Saginaw, MI. Capt. Bert Lambert was her captain, and I liked him.

**1955**     Early call, March 15—1st mate on the self-unloader Sierra, just purchased from the Tomlinson Steamship Company. She laid up December 20th. Capt. Art Hendrickson was her captain.

**1956**     Early again, March 15; laid up Dec. 22 in Fairport, OH. 1st mate with Capt. Galicky.

**1957**     Was called March 4 as 1st mate on the steamer Ben E. Tate, a self-unloader, with Capt. Kenneth Conn. He was an excellent captain. Then on July 25 I went captain until August 10; back to 1st mate until layup on December 20 in Milwaukee.

**1958**     Was called March 20 as 1st mate on the Sierra until we laid up December 21 in Fairport. Capt. Hendrickson was still her captain.

**1959**     Called March 26 as 1st mate on the Sierra again, with a new captain, Clarence A. McTevia. I liked him—an excellent ship-handler, very low-key, and never raised his voice.

**1960**     On March 24 went 1st mate on the Sierra again, at Milwaukee with Capt. Galicky until July 21, when I was transferred to the Joseph H. Frantz as 1st mate with Capt. Vernie Koski. Laid up in Milwaukee December 14.

**1961**     1st mate with Capt. Koski on the Joseph H. Frantz from March 18 to December 12, and laid her up in Milwaukee.

**1962**     On March 27 was called to go 1st mate on the Joseph H.

Frantz with Capt. Koski in Milwaukee; laid up December 5 in Superior, WI.

**1963**    April 1 was called to go 1st mate on the motor vessel (diesel) W. W. Holloway with Capt. McTevia. She had just been repowered and had new cabins. I really liked this boat. She also had a new bow thruster. We fit out in Lorain, OH.

**1964**    Early call on March 8, 1st mate on the self-unloader Crispin Oglebay, which I liked. She was equipped with a bow thruster. Her captain was Joe Galicky. We laid her up in Toledo December 20.

**1965**    Called March 15 as 1st mate on the Crispin Oglebay until July 15, then transferred to the E. G. Mathiott as 1st mate with Capt. Ernest McSorley in Toledo. We laid up in Chicago December 14.

**1965–66**    Went 3rd and 2nd mate on the car ferry City of Green Bay December 20, 1965, until March 1, 1966. Captain Eddie Erickson, her captain, was an excellent captain and boat-handler.

**1966**    Another early call, March 3 to July 10, as 1st mate with Captain McSorley on the repowered diesel-and converted Joseph H. Frantz with new cabins—really a nice boat. Got off her July 10 to go captain on the steamer Ben E. Tate July 12 in Lorain, OH. She was in dry dock. The mate said, "Shall I call for two tugs to depart?" I told him, "No, we'll try it by ourselves." We backed out, went up to the steel mill turn basin, turned and came on out without tugs. We laid her up in Toledo December 20.

**1967**    Called March 5 as captain on the steamer Wyandotte—a really nice boat and a good handler. We laid up in Toledo December 20.

**1968–69**    March 20 went captain on the Huron, a self-unloader and another good-handling boat. It was a bad season. We laid up June 15 in Wyandotte, and reported the next day as captain on the G. A. Tomlinson, serving on her until July 20, when her regular captain returned from sick leave in Toledo. Then went captain on the Wyandotte July 21 until September 20, when she went to Toledo for layup. So went master on the City of Milwaukee at Frankfort, MI Oct. 2. She was a railroad car ferry. Was on her until April 12, 1969, and was captain on the Arthur K. Atkinson and the City of Green Bay. I really enjoyed the car ferries—twin screws, nice cabins, and fun to handle. On April 15 I was appointed captain on the grain carrier James E. Ferris and liked her.

**1970** Back with Columbia April 10 in Fairport, OH as captain on the Crispin Oglebay, laid up in Lorain, OH December 22.

**1971** April 25 went captain on the grain carrier Kinsman Voyager until October 15, when I was transferred to the steamer Henry G. Steinbrenner as master, and laid her up in Cleveland December 10.

**1972** Appointed master on the Henry G. Steinbrenner on April 12 in Cleveland, and laid her up in Buffalo December 10. She was an excellent-handling boat.

**1973** Again appointed master on the Henry G. Steinbrenner on April 6 until May 2 in Cleveland, when I got off and went captain on the William A. Reiss May 4. She was a beautiful, nice-handling boat, equipped with a bow thruster and beautiful cabins. I laid this boat up in Toledo December 6.

**1974** Appointed captain on the steamer Merle M. McCurdy in Lorain, OH on April 8, and off again on April 30. Transferred to captain on the Frank R. Dentin in Toledo on May 6. Laid her up in Cleveland December 22, then transferred to the steamer Chicago Trader December 22 and laid up in Sandusky December 27 as captain.

**1975** April 8 was called to go captain on the Frank R. Dentin in

Cleveland until September 11 in Duluth; then transferred to the steamer Kinsman Enterprise September 12 as captain until October 16, when I was shifted to the steamer Ben Morrel October 17 until layup in Buffalo December 20.

**1976**    Appointed captain on the steamer Ben Morrel on April 12 until layup on December 1. This was a beautiful boat with nice cabins; she handled well.

**1977**    On April 8 was appointed master of the steamer Paul L. Tietjen until October 12, then transferred to the Henry G. Steinbrenner until December 21 as captain.

**1978–79**    April 9 the Kinsman Lines bought the Richard V. Lindabury and renamed her the Kinsman Independent. I was appointed her captain, and laid her up December 18. She was a beautiful-handling vessel. The mother of the mate on the Richard J. Reiss was dying and they couldn't get a relief mate, so on Dec. 18 I helped Boland out and took the Reiss as 1st mate until January 1, 1979. Then I went 1st mate on the motor vessel St. Clair from January 1–26, and laid up in Sturgeon Bay. That boat was cold. I threw the floor rugs across the bed to keep warm.

**1979–85**    I was on the Kinsman Independent as master, from fit-out 1978 through 1985. I really liked that vessel. She had no bow thruster, but I could take that 600-foot boat up the Lorain River, turn at the steel mill basin and come on out with no tug; go up and down the Buffalo River with no tug and turn at the turn basin with an anchor; or up and down the Calumet River in South Chicago, no tug; and in and out of the Alpena Cement dock without a tug. I never used any tugs around the grain elevators in Duluth, MN, Superior, WI or Thunder Bay, Ontario. She was a nice-handling boat and I had a steady, experienced crew.

# My Favorite Captains

## Captain John B. Routhier—Steamer International

Capt. Routhier was an excellent boat-handler, always low-key. I never heard him raise his voice.

I was his mate for six years and always wanted to shape my sailing career after his. He was a low-key man with a great sense of humor. I can't remember him ever swearing. He was a friendly man, but stayed pretty much to himself. He never mixed with the crew, but was there if he was needed. He never let the mates take over his job. When he was needed in the pilot house, he was there. One instance I can remember is when he had a bad case of the gout. He couldn't walk, but he'd climb up to the pilot house on his hands and knees to handle his boat. He was an extremely fine boat handler, and watched the weather closely. Capt. Routhier had three barometers, one in his bedroom, one in the office and, of course, one in the pilot house.

Capt. Routhier had a workshop in the fore-peak and spent a lot of time there, repairing furniture, making boat models and toys, etc. He seldom told anyone what he was building or for whom. I remember that once he made a big dollhouse. It was double-hinged so he could open the top to show all the tiny furniture he had made—bed, dresser, chairs, and so forth. Then he opened the other section to show the ground floor. When he got it all finished, painted and stowed in its own box with carrying handles, he gave it to Frank, the wheelsman, to take home to his two little girls.

Other items I remember him making were: a child's rocking chair, and an outboard motor boat 10 feet long. The boat was made entirely of oak, and all brass-screwed by hand. I believe I still have callouses from that job!

Capt. Routhier wanted no special treatment. He ate from the regular menu. He wore a suit and tie to all his meals; I never saw him in jeans.

Before we had radar, he'd call a ship equipped with radar and asked if he could follow closely on fogbound rivers. He requested that they call him if they checked speed. Today you can't run the rivers in the fog. The Coast Guard controls the rivers and puts you to anchor in fog, regardless of your equipment.

When he retired, Capt. Routhier bought the Colonial House on St. Ignace's Main Street, and added a motel behind it. Then he turned his large house into a bed and breakfast. He died some time ago, and then Mrs. Routhier also died. I'll never forget them.

## Captain Andy Greene

He was also a good boat-handler and seldom ever interfered with the mate's work. But as quiet as Capt. Greene was, you always knew he was master.

## Captain Bert Lambert

A soft-spoken little man, Capt. Lambert was always a gentleman. You felt you could discuss any problems with him. He treated us like family and always remembered birthdays with a card.

## Captain Clarence McTevia

He was quiet and kept to himself, but was always there if you needed him. In port he usually took a walk. Capt. McTevia seldom asked anyone to do anything for him, even pouring coffee.

## Captain Ernest McSorley

I believe I felt closer to Capt. McSorley than to any of the other captains. He never, ever discussed any problems with anyone. I knew him well and never knew any of his life before meeting him.

Still, I felt he had all the time in the world to listen to a problem. He never took chances, and was always studying the weather.

When they interviewed Nellie McSorley, Capt. McSorley's widow, about her life with the captain, she was on her death bed. Capt. McSorley had been captain on the Edmund Fitzgerald.

I sailed as Capt. McSorley's 1st mate on five different vessels. He was a nice, relaxed man who had time for everybody. I liked and respected him, but I always kept a little distance.

He told me once, at spring fit-out Coast Guard inspection, to always leave a few minor, trivial things undone so the inspector would have something to write about in his book. I always did, and believe me, it paid off.

We had a female 2nd mate once, and Capt. McSorley never called her by name. It was always "Mate." But he referred to all of his mates that way. In return, no one ever called him Ernie; it was always "Captain."

Just to illustrate the kind of person Capt. McSorley was:

We had a wheelsman who had a four-year-old adopted daughter who was to have a birthday in a couple of weeks. He was concerned that he was going to miss her party. So a few days before the party, Capt. McSorley put a deckhand on as temporary wheelsman and let the man off to attend her party. That wheelsman must have thanked the captain a dozen times. Payday came and he still received a full paycheck.

## Captain Eddie Erickson—the Ann Arbor Car Ferries

He was a nice captain. I was with him many times, and he always seemed pleased to see me. He was an excellent boat handler. He read a lot and always took long walks when we were in port.

After he retired from the railroad car ferries, he never passed through St. Ignace without stopping to visit or calling from his motel. His quarters on the boat were like a hospital room—spanking clean, with nothing lying around. I never, ever saw him needing a shave or a haircut, and never saw him angry.

## Captain William Bacon

Capt. Bacon was superintendent of the Ann Arbor car ferries out of Frankfort, MI, and an excellent man to work for. Capt. Bacon was "all business," never talkative, but was behind you if you happened to need a favor.

Many of the local crew occasionally took their wives for a trip across the lake that lasted 12 hours or so. One day I asked another captain if it was all right for me to take my wife along on a trip or two. He asked, "Do you have five years seniority?" I told him, "No, I've got about five weeks." He said, "Ask again when you've got five years."

When I told Capt. Bacon my problem he said, "You've got a Catholic name, and he hates Catholics. Use my phone and tell your wife to plan on a couple of weeks." So I did.

Capt. Bacon asked his secretary to make me a permanent railroad pass to include meals and room. The pass, encased in plastic, was not to be surrendered. I thought the other captain was going to have a baby when my wife presented him the pass. He handed it back to her and left, never saying "enjoy your trip" or anything. Word must have gotten around, because Lou made many trips after that and never even had to show her railroad pass.

Ann Arbor #4 —1900 —1973 —73yrs.

# Galley Stories

When I was 1st mate on the self-unloader E. G. Mathiott in 1947, our captain was a six-foot four-inch man from Beaver, IL., and really strict.

During one meal, he rapped on the table and the 2nd cook came in. The captain said, "Tell the steward to come in here." So the cook came in and the captain said, "Can you bake pies?" The cook said, "Yes, Sir, yes, Sir." The captain slapped the table about six times and said, "I want pie on this table six times a week, and Sunday with whipped cream on it." The cook said, "Yes, Sir," and scooted back into the galley.

So that cook had pie seven days a week, and never changed the flavor—huckleberry pies every day. It'd be piled up on the table for night lunch, and each night the clean-up man threw it over the side.

Once when I was going aft for my breakfast, the captain hollered for a toasted sausage sandwich. When I came back I discovered that the cook had rotated his breakfast meat; that day he had bacon. So he made a bacon sandwich for the captain. I brought him the sandwich and he told me to watch the boat while he had his sandwich and coffee. When he saw that bacon, he threw it on the deck, jumped on it, and said, "You go back and get me a sausage sandwich, whether he's got sausage or not." I went down and went to bed.

I was on a boat where the 2nd cook would save the sausage and bacon grease for our 2nd assistant engineer, who was about 5-foot 5 and weighed well over 200 pounds. He'd come up to the galley, grab three or four slices of homemade bread, soak them in the grease. When the bread was gone he'd drink the rest of the grease; died when he was about 45.

One time when I was captain, our 1st mate's wife and 12-year-old daughter were making a trip with us on the girl's birthday. The 2nd cook baked a nice cake and had it decorated. After the noon meal, they did an excellent job of decorating the dining room. The cook went out of his way to prepare a turkey dinner with all the trimmings, and also had a decorated basket sitting on the back counter where the crew put gifts for the girl. When she and her folks arrived for dinner, everyone yelled "Surprise!" and sang "Happy Birthday" to Tracy. The cook struck the bell 12 times in her honor.

We were going to be out in Lake Superior at meal time on that birthday, and there were northwesterly winds at about 30 miles per hour. It wasn't too rough, but would be uncomfortable for a party. So I checked down and came slowly up the river, then anchored for about an hour and a half behind Whitefish Point, faking an engine breakdown. Everything went beautifully. I don't know if the little girl knew about the party ahead of time, but she acted surprised. Every once in a while there was a little "home life" on those big boats.

When I was watching on the steamer Augustus B. Wolvin, the first 600-foot all-steel freighter, we had a couple from Ashtabula, the cook and 2nd cook. The cook was about five-foot-eight and weighed about 160 pounds. His wife was about five-foot-ten and weighed over 400 pounds. She waddled when she walked. In the spring, at "fit-out" time, we'd lower the dock's 17-ton-capacity unloading clam on the dock, she'd step in and they'd hoist her aboard. She never left the ship all season, and nine months later, in December at layup time, they would use the same device to lower her to the dock.

During the season, she 'most always peeled her vegetables while sitting on a pair of steel bitts, stern of the cabin. These bitts were about eight inches in diameter, about eight inches apart, and

94

about 20 inches high; they were used to moor or tie the vessel to the dock. She had a 2 x 4 rug she'd toss over the bitts and sit on that.

The cook was short-tempered and mean, but his wife was always jolly and a really nice person. We just couldn't do enough for her. She liked candy and we, the crew, always brought her some when we came back from shore leave. I remember the first time I saw her underpants hanging on the line; they were huge and looked like sails.

Years ago there were many combination teams, man and wife as 1st cook and 2nd cook. That, too, seems to be a thing of the past. I am guessing, but I'd say the union's perhaps responsible for that, as both husband and wife would have to have equal seniority, to rate the same ship.

We had a cooking team, a man and wife, on the steamer at the end of the season. They quit sailing and bought the Dry Dock Tavern in River Rouge, MI. An old man hung around there wearing a heavy winter overcoat year 'round. So the cook told him he'd fix up a cot for him in the basement. He installed a shower and toilet, cook stove and refrigerator, and told him, "You can stay down here rent-free if you clean and mop the tavern after closing time."

During the day he'd eat upstairs with them. He never took his heavy overcoat off. This went on for about five years, and he died leaving no relatives.

He left everything to the cook and his wife. His overcoat was lined with thousands of dollars. He had four or five apartment houses and a great deal of stock. All told, he left about $850,000; no one thought he was worth a dime.

The cook closed the tavern, bought a large, well-equipped van and traveled around the country for about a year. He became tired of that and returned to Detroit, opened up his tavern again.

We didn't have refrigeration on the boats for some time after I started sailing. So every time we got groceries, we'd get huge cakes of ice for our walk-in refrigerator. On sunny days we'd take turns crank-ing the ice cream maker in the middle of a barrel on the last hatch.

When we'd get our groceries aboard the boats, it'd be a couple quarters of beef, half a pig, half a mutton, a bushel of mixed fruit, and maybe a half bushel oranges or apples, three times a week. Along with our groceries would be 10 large ice cubes (15") for our ice box. Often we got fish, fresh and in the round. The galley would have to kill and clean them. We'd sometimes buy fresh rabbit, beaver, venison and even porcupine for a wild meat supper.

One cook I really liked was Orville Wollan from Sault Ste. Marie, MI. He was only about 21 or 22, and an excellent cook. He was always dressed in white. His bills at the end of the month were usually the lowest in the fleet, but I am sure his crew ate the best. We ex-change holiday cards and occasionally I run into him at the Sault. He retired after I did and still lives in the Sault.

Our cook, Val, was married and lived in Duluth, but he had a **girlfriend.** One day en route to Superior, we ran into strong head winds, **so were** delayed for about three hours. Val got all dolled up, and we just knew he was seeing his girlfriend that night. He always walked looking down, so when he came to the office shore gate, he looked up and there were his wife and his girlfriend, sitting together, waiting for him. The women didn't know they were both waiting for Val. When he saw them, he took off on a run, back to the boat. Never did hear how he solved that problem.

Val was often half under the weather on the boat. The galley crew claimed he mixed vanilla with cider, and called it apple jack. So this one day I saw Val coming up the deck with a rolled paper in his hand. I told Frankie, my wheelsman, "I'll bet you 50 cents the first item on the cook's grocery list is a large bottle of vanilla." Frankie said, "You're on."

The cook had the captain sign a requisition for groceries. When he came into the pilot house and started to fill his pipe, I quickly grabbed his grocery order. He chased me around the wheel a couple of times, then sat down. I looked at his list, and the very first item was: 2 large bottles of vanilla. I won the 50 cents.

Our cook once missed the boat, and an oiler came up to me and said, "Captain, the cook missed her, who's going to do the cooking?" I told him, "You are, and the first one who complains is automatically the next cook." The next day I asked him, "Did you have any complaints?" He said, "The watchman said, 'This meat is tough. . .but it's sure good'—he caught himself just in time."

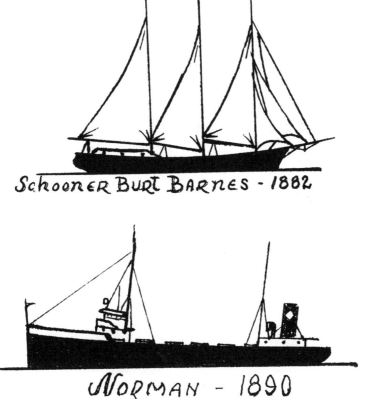

Schooner Burt Barnes - 1882

Norman - 1890

# The Cygnus / The Canopus

My first job on a lake freighter was deck-watch on the Cygnus, a 425-foot freighter. It was also that captain's first command. He was six-foot-two and weighed about 350. He would eat his meal and then have the cook make him a couple of sandwiches for a later lunch.

Walking on the deck, he'd go only about 100 feet and then had to sit on a hatch and rest for a bit. We had a violent storm and I got seasick. I recall that the next morning he asked me if I had been seasick. I said, "Sure was, Captain." He said, "Don't feel bad. I get seasick every time we have a storm." He was 48 then, and died when he was 50.

His son was captain on the Interlake fleet many years later.

At the end of the 1938 season I was packing to leave the Cygnus for home when the captain of the steamer Canopus, a boat 463 feet long and 50 feet wide, asked me if I'd like another three weeks of work on her. I did, and we laid up in South Chicago on December 16, 1938. I was really proud to be a sailor.

We carried mostly iron ore and grain, with an occasional cargo of coal. To keep the cargo from getting wet, our hatches were nearly always covered with canvas tarps, which were about 40' x 10' and heavy.

I remember the captains of these boats. The captain of the Cygnus was a huge man, as I have said. The captain of the Canopus was about five-feet-ten, a neat dresser, and his penmanship was really beautiful. He once told me that to be really good at anything, all you had to do was practice, practice and practice—so ever since then, I've been practicing writing.

# The Augustus B. Wolvin

or three years early in my career I was assigned to the steamer Augustus B. Wolvin, the first 600-foot vessel built for the lakes, 540 feet long and 56 feet wide, with 16 hatches. She had been built in 1904 for the Interlake Steamship Company and was 540 x 56 x 32, with 16 hatches. Her hull was painted yellow and she was dubbed The Yellow Kid. But that was before my time. When I worked on her, she was iron ore red. I was a watchman the first year and a wheelsman the next two years.

Wheeling on the Wolvin, I once saw the captain pass out when we were about half a boat length from entering the Poe Lock at Sault Ste. Marie. I dragged him to the middle of the floor where he could lie comfortably while I steered her into the lock, and called the lockmaster for a doctor. By the time we tied up, the doctor was waiting for us.

The problem was that the captain had been wearing tight support socks and they had cut off his circulation. The doctor pulled the socks down to the captain's ankles and he was all right. Captain thanked me for not making a big thing out of the situation.

In 1940, I was wheeling on the Wolvin when we had that terrible Armistice Day storm. My closest buddy, Walter Kewise, went down in that storm on the William B. Davock off Pentwater, MI. All hands were lost—27 men—along with those of two other steamers, the Anna Minch and the Novadoc, all in the same vicinity on Lake Michigan. Details of that storm are given in the section of this book dealing with shipwrecks.

The Wolvin's captain was a six-foot Norwegian, a really nice guy. I liked and respected him. Our 1st mate was a little high strung man, and always worked his watch from 2 to 6 a.m. and p.m.

This mate had a habit of changing course often—one or two degrees one way or the other, then back again. One day as we came down Lake Superior on a nice, calm day, I steadied the boat and then took the two-inch hub nut off the middle of the wheel, lifted the wheel off and leaned it against the chart table while the mate was looking out the front window. When he turned around and found me in back of the wheel house with the steering wheel in front of me, I thought he was going to go right through the roof.

Another time, around 3 a.m., the mate was pouring coffee and asked if I'd like a cup. I told him yes, and to toss a little cream and sugar in it. He said, "I'll pour your coffee, but if you want to doctor it up, that's your job. I wouldn't spoil coffee for anyone." I started drinking it black then, and still do.

One morning he asked me, "Do you and your wife ever argue?" I told him that we did occasionally, just like all couples. He said that one night he and his wife were arguing before bedtime. When they went to bed, she climbed over to her side as far as she could, and he did the same on his side. In the morning he spoke to her and she didn't answer. He touched her shoulder and found she had died during the night. He never got over that. Some time later he married again, and if they ever argue they always kiss and make up before going to sleep.

Years later I was captain and he was dispatcher for salt water vessels at Port Huron. He called me and said, "Captain, keep that wheel on the stand."

In his later years he was a captain, and had a severe heart attack. The company told him he had a lifetime job as 1st mate, but not to ever plan on a captain's job again.

In 1939, when I was wheelsman on the Wolvin, we had a chief engineer who had his wife on board for a trip in mid-October, as this was his last trip, and he was going to retire when they got back to Toledo.

The after-cabin was the engineer's gang's living quarters. In the fantail, aft of the engine room, they have "gang-way doors" that open like Dutch doors—2 half-doors, both about 4 feet x 4 feet. In port they usually have the top half open.

This particular day, at Superior, WI, we had just loaded iron ore and were backing down the dock. Near the end of the dock was a set of bare post pilings, protruding from the water against the dock to a height of about 12 feet, wrapped together with steel cable. The chief's wife was standing on the main deck talking to the chief, who had his upper body protruding out from the gangway. He was looking forward as the ship was moving astern.

They came upon the pilings and sheared his head right off.

About that time, a drunken fireman came back to the ship a little late, picked up the head, tucked it under his arm and came up the ladder. He laid the head on the hatch cover and went back to his room.

I didn't witness this mishap, and was glad that I had not.

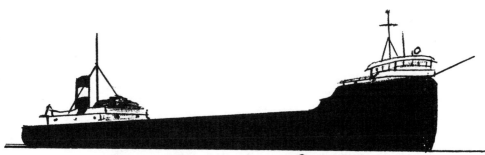

*Augustus B. Wolvin*
540' x 56' x 32'

# William F. Stifel

O n April 1, 1953, I was assigned as 1st mate on the William F. Stifel. Her captain was Ernest McSorley. I liked him and was glad to get off the Mathiott. We had an uneventful year, laying up in Buffalo on December 17. Capt. McSorley was a gentleman. I was with him again on the Mathiott, the Sierra and Joe Frantz. Of all the captains I was ever with, I'd say he was the best all-around captain.

On his last trip upbound through the Sault Locks, I talked to him for about 15 seconds, and before hanging up I said, "Good luck in the lake, Captain. She's blowing pretty good." He said, "Thanks, I need all the luck I can get. The chief engineer, 1st mate, 1st assistant engineer and I are all going to retire together when we get back to Toledo."

They never made it. I got chills down my back for the next two years when I passed the spot where they went down. They were on the Edmund Fitzgerald.

I remember telling Capt. McSorley once how I'd lost my rosary. A couple of weeks later I came into my room and there was a new black rosary on my desk with a note saying, "Try not to lose this." I still have it.

The reason I'd lost my rosary was that I was trying to ship out in the early spring and hadn't eaten for a couple of days, so about 5 p.m. one day I knocked on the rectory door of St. Peter & Paul's Church in South Chicago. A big, fat priest smoking a cigar came to the door and said, "What can I do for you, Son?" I told him I hadn't eaten for two days, and that I was from upper Michigan and trying to ship out on a boat.

I could smell the pork chops cooking. He said, "Are you from this church?" I told him, "No; if I was I'd be home." He said, "When you are, come back and we'll see if we can help you." I said, "The hell with you." I showed him my rosary and then threw it down the alley. Later I found out that every morning he had his breakfast rolls, milk and cream delivered about 4:30 a.m. on his back porch . . . so I saw to it that the priest went without his breakfast for quite a few mornings. I never went regularly, so they never caught me.

While I was 1st mate on the William F. Stifel, the 3rd assistant engineer asked the captain if his wife could make a trip. The captain said, "Sure, make sleeping arrangements." I had a double bed, and the engineer shared a room with twin beds. So I offered my room and took his room.

After one seven-day trip, he asked if she could make another trip, and the captain said okay. We got up to Duluth and the captain got a shore phone call from the 3rd engineer's wife, who wanted to know if her husband was okay; he hadn't sent his check home. They had two children and lived in Marine City. So the always-obliging captain blew his stack. He came back to the boat and paid the engineer off, telling him to get off the boat right now. I was pleased, and got my bed back. He hadn't even thanked me for the swap.

~ William F. Stifel ~

# The J. L. Mauthe

*I*'d never criticize another captain's judgment. He didn't get to be a captain by being lucky. Captains all have paid their dues and earned their jobs. There's no way any captain can judge the weather and always be 100% right. Even today with modern satellite equipment, the weather stations are often wrong.

One night the J. L. Mauthe and my ship, the Kinsman Independent, left Superior at about the same time, with grain for the same elevator in Buffalo. The wind was a northeasterly gale and the Mauthe hugged the north shore, bound for anchorage in Thunder Bay, Ontario.

I had a Grundig shortwave radio in the pilot house, and found through some of the shore stations inland that the wind was shifting to southeast, so I headed for Keweenaw Waterway, taking me through Hancock and Houghton. I figured that if the wind didn't go southeast, I'd have excellent anchorage, and if it did, I'd keep going and follow the south shore in the lee of the land to Whitefish Point.

We rolled pretty hard until we reached the upper entrance of the waterway. Three hours later the wind went southeast; I sailed on to Whitefish and had pretty good going. Quite a few boats were anchored in Thunder Bay. We stayed off the radio, and by the time they were aware of the wind change, we had a long lead on them.

We beat the Mauthe to Buffalo, and the Mauthe had to anchor for two days until we cleared. That time I had guessed right, but along the way I also made a lot of wrong guesses.

# The Richard V. Lindabury

The Kinsman Lines, owned by New York Yankees' George Steinbrenner, purchased the Richard V. Lindabury in early 1978 and renamed her the Kinsman Independent. She was 600' x 60'. I was her skipper from 1978-1985 when she was named the Kinsman Independent. She was built in 1923, and was a beautiful-handling ship. I seldom used tugs.

When I retired my 1st mate got to sail her. On November 24, 1989, she went aground off Isle Royale. According to the Coast Guard inquest, the normal charted lake carriers' course is just east of the island. The boat went aground 24 miles west of the charted course about 11 a.m., and the weather was clear.

The captain was in control and fetched up, going full speed, about 14 M.P.H. They were en route to Thunder Bay, Ontario for grain. Thunder Bay Shipyard revealed 5,000 square feet of damage to hull plates and further damage to framing and forward ballast tanks. Kinsman Lines' loss was Thunder Bay Shipyard's gain, as the yard had little drydock work. They called back 50 workers and took about six weeks for the $1.5 million repair job.

The Coast Guard inquest revealed human error. She was equipped with all modern navigational equipment, yet slammed into the island at noon in clear weather. And—get this—he was back on board as captain the following spring.

And George Steinbrenner had nearly fired me because I had too much postage on a letter. He bought me a $30 postage scale, with orders to use it.

# The Sierra

*I* was 1st mate on the self-unloader *Sierra*, and next in line for a captain's job. We used to run into Saginaw quite a bit with stone and coal. The grocery man would come aboard with a box of candy for the captain and a paper. He'd meet me often on deck and ignore me completely, never a "hi" or a wave or anything.

One time we swapped captains and he drove our captain up to Rogers City to catch his new boat at midnight. So I got a call to get off the boat in Saginaw to catch my new boat at the Ford plant in Detroit. She'd be due out at 7 a.m.

We got tied up about 10 p.m. and I was read to go. I met the grocery man at the ladder and told him, "I have to catch a boat at Detroit; how about a ride?" He said, "It's 10 o'clock; I can't take you there." So I contacted a couple of bars and found an unemployed guy who said that if I didn't mind his wife and daughter coming, he'd take me. So I gave him $50 and paid for his gas and oil. He was glad to take me.

About a month later, as captain, I came into Saginaw with a load of stone. The same grocery man came aboard with his candy and paper, talked for a bit and then said, "Well, I guess I'll go back and see the cook." (Before his arrival I had told the cook, "This man gets no grocery order, ever.") I said, "You can visit the cook if you wish, but you may recall that I didn't get transportation from you, so you'll never get a grocery order from us." He never returned—but he did leave his paper and candy.

We used to deal with an old-time marine grocery man when in Duluth. On my first trip to Duluth as captain, a new, young marine grocery man came down and asked if he could share our grocery order. I told him we always got our fresh fish from the Odanwa Indian Reservation, but if he'd store and deliver their fish to us, he could have all of our grocery business. So he gained a new customer and I found a new friend. He was a hard worker and really nice. He often left his car for me on the dock, but I never used it. I received a Christmas card from him long after I retired, but don't anymore.

While I was working my way up in my sailing career, I saw so much drinking, partying and injuries because of the drinking, I swore that when I got to be 1st mate I would run a tight ship. The 1st mate usually runs the work and crew.

When I was appointed 1st mate, and for the rest of my career, I stuck to that promise. I know I wasn't the most popular mate or captain, but I usually had the best safety record.

When I was mate on the Sierra, the captain had the same drinking crew for four or five years. Our first trip into Port Washington, one of the senior watchmen came back from shore leave with a shopping bag full of booze. I met him at the ladder and told him, "You can come aboard, but you can't bring the booze." He ignored me and carried his bag up the ladder. I took the bag away from him, tossed it over the side, and told him, "You're fired." He said, "I'll see the captain about that."

He trotted up to the captain's office, and the captain told him, "If the mate fired you, you're fired." The rest of the crew got the message, and turned out to be a good crew.

We laid the Sierra up in Sturgeon Bay, WI one year, and had to take a local bus to get transportation out of Green Bay. I was 1st mate, and our ship's pilot house clock—a Chelsea Ship's Bell Clock, worth about $300 at that time (about $600 today) had been missing. We were all waiting at the bus station when 7 p.m. came, and the ship's bell in the watchman's sea bag struck the time. The captain fired the watchman right there, and retrieved the clock.

# *The Ben E. Tate*

*I*n 1964, *I was captain on the steamer Ben E. Tate,* a Columbia self-unloader. We were northbound on Lake Michigan following the east shore, and the wind was strong and northeasterly.

The wind shifted to northwest and really started blowing hard. I went into South Manitou harbor, about 200 feet offshore. It was like a millpond in there, like a mirror.

The mate came into my room and asked if three or four of the crew could lower a lifeboat and go ashore to get a Christmas tree and if Joe could take his .22 long rifle, which I stowed in my locked locker. (He had won the rifle in a raffle.)

So ashore they went. They came back about four hours later with three or four Christmas trees, a deer and two rabbits. One of the trees was huge, so they set it up in front of the smokestack. Later, after a shopping spree, they had the tree fully decorated. It looked great. We got quite a few phone calls complimenting us on our nice tree.

The boys had a cleaning party, skinned and cut up the rabbits and deer. So we had a few unplanned nice meals. We stayed anchored for two days, then left. That was the only time I ever anchored there; it's too small a harbor for a really large freighter, but being only 450 feet, we found that it suited us just fine.

On the Tate, our unloading boom was about 180 feet long and reached right to our after cabin. It had about an eight-foot chute on the end, hinged so that if we wanted to throw coal or stone a little farther on the docks, we'd lower this chute, and it would throw coal another 10 or 12 feet.

While loading coal cargo, I'd have the mate leave the last two hatches open and pile an extra car of coal high on deck. After the fuel bunker got down about 60 tons, we'd have a fuel party, hoist the boom up, lower the chute, and fill the fuel bunker with the coal cargo. We'd clean up the deck, rinse her down, and continue on our way with our fuel bunker full of cheap coal. Luckily, no one squealed, because we never got caught, although we didn't do that too often.

While I was sailing the Tate en route to Marblehead, OH (near Sandusky) to load stone, ahead of me I heard two Canadians talking. One of them said he was going to Marblehead to load stone. I felt I could beat him, so I called the chief and told him to start pumping out the ballast and open her up full speed. The normal route is to leave Kelly Island on your right. So I charted a short cut course to leave Green Island and Kelly Island on my left, passing over a 15-foot shoal.

When approaching the shoal, I stopped the engine and ballast pumps, and coasted over the shoal. About a mile ahead and to my right was the stone dock. About two miles ahead was the Canadian. I knew I had him, so gave a security call: "Steamer Ben E. Tate, en route to the Marblehead stone dock." The Canadian captain, excited, called and said he was going to the stone dock. I told him, "You'll have to wait your turn." He anchored for nine hours until we had loaded and departed. Needless to say, I didn't make any brownie points with that captain.

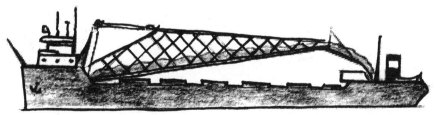

Stmr. Ben E. Tate filling fuel bunker

# *The Harvester*

*Y*ears before I got on the *Harvester*, she was down-bound at the Sault once with a whole slew of traffic ahead of her. The captain figured that if he took the Canadian lock, he'd bypass much of that traffic. In a hurry, he shot for the Canadian lock, could not stop her in time, and knocked the lower gates down. So he and the lock water went out together. He did get a little bottom damage, but was able to continue on to Chicago.

I was 2nd mate in 1946 on the Harvester. As we left the Wisconsin Steel Mill slip in South Chicago, the deck watch (with a red wave flashlight) was signaling the watchman, who was operating the steam deck winch. While closing the hatches, he stumbled on a stray hatch clamp at 1 a.m. and fell in the cargo hold, 40 feet down to the cargo deck.

I saw this red flashlight make two large circles on the way down, and just before he hit the deck he extended both arms to break his fall. He wound up with a broken jaw, broken collar bone, and broken hip. We called an ambulance and hoisted him onto a stretcher.

He was discharged from the hospital 11 months later. He had small children, so about twice a month his wife would get $100 to survive (his potential settlement from the lawyer). His lawyer finally told him all he could get for him was $35,000, minus the money he had advanced his family. He told the lawyer "No way," he'd take the $35,000, no strings attached. So after 11 months in the hospital, all he got was $35,000. Incidentally, he died of a heart attack the summer of 1994.

My last year with the Harvester we had a captain they had hired from the Hutchinson Company. This new captain was going to change all of our mates with mates from his former company. Knowing this, I watched my step.

I got the season in all right and then kept ship all winter. Shipkeeper is like a babysitter on a boat. (Insurance companies demand that a man remain aboard all year in case of problems with weather, fire or foul play.) The company was aware that I was planning to change companies in the spring. However, no one else knew.

Along towards spring, one Saturday afternoon at 5 p.m. I heard a knock on my door. A truck driver was there with a note from the captain: "Assist truck driver–load 10 hatch canvas tarps." No reason given, nothing. So I asked the truck driver his name, address, phone number, driver's license and truck license numbers. Then I assisted him with the 10 tarps, knowing he was from the captain's hometown in Wisconsin.

About a month later the tarps were not returned. I figured the captain sold them. So I put together all the information I had and brought it to the marine office. I left the company shortly after that, but did hear later that the company made the captain replace those 10 tarps. Each was about 50 feet by 12 feet, and worth about $80 per tarp.

"Nevada" America's 1st "Roll-on-Roll-off"

~ Arthur K. Atkinson ~
Ann Arbor rail road car ferry--384' × 56' × 20' 6"

# The International / The A. A. Augustus

*n the late 30s I got hold of a used mate's corres-*pondence course and studied for those two years, then wrote the Coast Guard Marine exam and got my mate's license. The next spring, in 1941, I went 3rd mate on International Harvester's ship the International, a really nice ship 600 feet long, 60 feet wide and 30 feet deep. My wheelsman was a veteran, having had about 20 years of wheeling time, so I felt comfortable with him on watch. In fact, if I wanted to change course or seek advice, I'd timidly ask him.

After the first couple of days, on our first trip to Duluth for ore, I asked him something and he said, "Mate, you've got the license; you're the boss here. I am part of your crew, your wheelsman. If you want something, tell me, don't ask. We're a team and I won't let you down." The man was my wheelsman for three years. I learned a great deal from him and respected him.

Our captain, Capt. Andrew Greene, was in his 60s, a low-key person who never raised his voice. If he needed to give you advice, he always called you aside, and almost always worked through his mates, seldom ever giving the crew a direct order. He'd tell the mates what he wanted and they'd relay his wishes to the crew.

I remember once that we had a new cook who fixed pork chops and fried potatoes for supper. The 2nd cook brought the captain a big t-bone steak and a baked potato. He asked the 2nd cook to send the cook in to see him, and when the cook arrived the captain said, "Steward, take this steak back to the galley. Hereafter, I eat exactly what the crew eats."

The captain told me once, "Never cheat on help. If you've got a two- or three-man job, it's better to have an extra man to do the job than to be a man short." I always followed his advice.

In 1942, before the Coast Guard monitored the rivers, the A. A. Augustus and the International were running together from Chicago to Duluth. The Augustus had radar; The International didn't. Approaching the Straits, eastbound, our captain called the Augustus and told the captain that fog was setting in, and we would stay about 500 feet behind him and follow him through the Straits and up the rivers. We told him to let us know if he planned on checking. We followed the Augustus up the fogbound rivers, through the Locks and up Lake Superior.

Sometimes we'd barely see him; but everything went fine.

When I was 2nd mate on the International, on our first trip down, at Whitefish we noted a lot of ice and a whole string of boats ahead of us. We didn't have a radio telephone, so the captain telegraphed the Sault Coast Guard and asked if he could swing around the boats ahead, which were all in a single line. They told him he could pass anything up to the Gros Cap light ship, so he swung out of the line and passed about 15 ships. Most of them had radio telephones and were really calling us, other boats, and the Coast Guard.

We slid into line at the light ship. We had a shortwave radio in the pilot house, so could hear all the calls.

We finally got a radio telephone about 1944.

Ore was scarce, so we got a few stray loads of grain and stone to fill in. En route for our first load of grain, the mate had a heart attack. We put him off at Marquette and continued on to Superior to load our grain. The 2nd mate was a nervous type of a guy and had never been on a grain boat. The captain told this 2nd mate, "John, you're our new mate until our mate gets back. The 2nd mate said, "No, Sir, Captain; I'll get off before I go 1st mate." Then the captain turned to me and said, "How about you, Ray?" I had been 3rd mate for only about four months, but I said, "Yes, Sir, I'd like to give her a try." So we got a temporary 3rd mate and I went 1st mate for the remaining five months of the season.

I could never thank that 1st mate, now captain, enough for that loading book. The captain told me, "Don't hesitate to call me if you're stuck." Luckily, I never had to call him. Everything went fine. I went 2nd mate the next spring.

At the end of my third year on that ship (one year as 3rd mate, two years as 2nd mate) the captain called me into his office. I was only 25 years old. He said, "How'd you like to be 1st mate next spring?" I said, "Fine." He told me the 1st mate had been bypassed for the captain's job on the Harvester and was quitting the company at the end of the season.

You had to have a Master's License to sail as mate; in case something happened to the captain, you could take over. He said, "Get the license and the job's yours." I wrote to all the Coast Guard Marine Inspection offices on the lakes. They all told me I'd have to have three years as 2nd mate or one year as 1st mate to write for a master's license.

Then I got a reply from Captain McMaster from the Chicago office. He said he'd count my 3rd mate's time as 2nd mate, because of the mate shortage—and I could write, with proof of my time. I enrolled in the Lake Carriers Navigation School and in the spring secured my license. I was elated, and waiting eagerly for spring.

One week before fit-out, my captain called and said, "The mate's job is yours, but...I just got a call from Herb, the mate who quit. His father died and his wife had a stroke. He wants his job back. But it's up to you."

I told him, "I've got lots of time; Herb hasn't. I'll stay 2nd mate."

*(The International is pictured on page 168.)*

115

# The Ben Morrel

*I*t was on the steamer *Ben Morrel* and we were west of Isle Royale, bound for Duluth, and keeping about three miles off the north shore. We had a northwesterly gale blowing about 45 miles per hour, and were riding comfortably when on my radio I heard a couple of boats talking. One of them said, "This wind has peaked, with gusts up to 80 miles per hour."

About that time I had 50 miles per hour and was off a high shore bluff. So I checked her right down and headed for the shoreline. I planned on going in dead slow until my fathometer (water depth meter) showed about 20 feet, then drop the hook (anchor).

The water remained deep, and I was only about 200 feet off the beach, so I was going to drop the hook when she stopped. I had run into the bank all of a sudden. She lay still, so I backed off. She moved right away, so again I rammed the bank, put her on slow speed, and lay there for about 10 hours—when the weather started clearing up and the wind dropped to about 30 miles per hour—before backing off. We had lain there nicely, so I marked the spot on the chart and told a few other captains about it. We had a comfortable run to Duluth. Thankfully, I never had to use that spot again.

My 1st mate was a very high-strung person. His daughter, mother-in-law and son-in-law were meeting the boat to have dinner with him. He was hurrying to get dressed while I talked to his family. He finally came hurrying on deck in shirt, tie, blazer and shoes—all dressed up—with no pants on. He took a lot of ribbing over that.

I was captain on the Ben Morrel and, while docking at Port Washington, my deckhand put the eye of the mooring cable on the dock spile, but was not using the cable becket. The cable winch got a backlash and started to take in on the cable, taking three of the deckhand's fingers off. The eye of the cable was on the dock spile, holding the deckhand's canvas glove.

I had the watchman slack off on the cable, removed the canvas glove with the three fingers in it, and rushed the man to the hospital where his three fingers were re-attached. My deckhand was back sailing the next year—with working fingers.

*Ben Morrel - 1922*

E.G. Mathiott
353′ × 48.2 × 28′

# The E. G. Mathiott /
# The Carrollton /
# The R. E. Moody

*I* was appointed 1st mate on the Columbia self-unloader E. G. Mathiott, and arrived aboard in Fairport, OH. We were fitting out and getting the ship ready to sail. The second day of work, the captain walked up to me with two water glasses half full of booze. He handed me a glass and said, "Here, Mate, to a good season." I said, "I am sorry, Captain, but I don't drink aboard a boat." He looked at me really hard and said, "You'll drink it or you'll wear it!" I said, looking him right in the eyes, "I am not drinking it, and I am not wearing it!"

He took his two glasses back up to his quarters and never bothered me about drinking again. I ran a tight ship, but I couldn't stop the captain from drinking. I told the crew that anyone caught drinking aboard was automatically fired. My crew had the best safety record in the fleet.

Another time, same captain, same ship—while unloading in Cleveland, I told the 2nd mate, "Put one set of tarps off to be repaired." We had two full sets aboard. So I was relieved and went to bed. We were loading three days later in Grand Haven with the captain again up the street. I went up to the pilot house to get the 6 p.m. weather report: Strong northwesterly gales 50+ miles per hour. So I came down on deck and told the watchman to call some extra men out and have the tarps ready to put on. He came back to me and said, "Mate, there's not a tarp aboard." The 2nd mate had put both sets of tarps off in Cleveland. We had a full gale coming up and no tarps for our wooden hatches.

Now, that captain was a hard-headed man; you don't tell him

what to do. So knowing how he'd react, I met him when he came aboard just before we loaded. Seeing he was well under the weather, I said strongly, "I don't care what you think, Captain—I am going to call extra men out on overtime and get the tarps out. We have storm warnings." He said, ""You will like hell. I'll tell you what to do. We don't need no tarps!" I waited until he was halfway up the deck going to the pilot house, caught up to him again and said, "I still think we should haul those tarps out." He said, "Forget those tarps and get off my back!" Exactly what I wanted. We had to head right into the wind and sea, and reach the west shore before we could start up the lake. He never knew we didn't have a tarp aboard.

Another time, same captain, same ship — on a holiday, we were tied up at the T.O.T. dock in Toledo. I was in the galley having a cup of coffee. We had all the hatches open, ready to load coal in the morning. The 2nd mate ran back to the galley and said, "The captain wants you right away," so I started walking up the deck. Captain had a three-foot megaphone, standing near his door, yelling, "When I call you, you MOVE." I kept walking the same pace, and when I got near enough so he could hear me, told him, "If you want me to move faster, call me earlier." He got so mad he threw the megaphone in the cargo hold, slammed the door and went into his room. I never did learn what he wanted.

In spite of all his drinking, he had very few mishaps.

The spring of 1948, I was assigned 3rd mate with Captain Andrew Greene, a native of Beaver Island. I had relatives on that island, so we got along very well. On the self-unloader E. G. Mathiott, a boat with 10 wooden hatches that was 353 x 48.3 x 28, we made a lot of smaller ports that larger boats couldn't handle. Our captain was an extremely good boat handler, and I bought a leather notebook to keep notes on tips he gave me and things he did. I added tips all during my sailing career. I haven't seen that notebook for some time now, but it's somewhere around my house.

When we were on our way to Oswego, NY we were delayed

three days because of a storm. Our fuel was beginning to run low, so while we unloaded coal I lowered the extended spout on the end of the unloading boom, raised the boom about 40 feet, and positioned it in the middle of the coal bunker. I started unloading and hit the bunker about right, putting about 30 tons of coal in it. . .not too good a grade, but enough to get us back to Toledo. I told the dock foreman and he said, "That's okay. Glad to be able to help." He had a huge stockpile on the dock.

We laid up in Fairport, OH on December 12, 1948, and that winter I spent on the Lake Michigan car ferries out of Frankfort, MI. There were six ferries and, being a relief man, I was jumping from boat to boat.

In 1954, I was assigned again to the E. G. Mathiott as 1st mate with Captain McSorley, until October 18 when I was transferred to the Carrollton until layup on December 16. The company's senior captain, Bert Lambert, was her captain—a really nice guy. I was pleased to be with him. I learned a lot from him, and he gave me many tips which I wrote down in my notebook. I often referred to this book of tips, even after I got my captain's job.

The Carrollton was 247.5 x 43.2 x 21.6. She had two huge hatches and carried mostly steel products from Saginaw to Buffalo. She spent a lot of time in port and had an old, steady crew. Captain Lambert was her captain in 1954, and I was her 1st mate. He had to get off for about a week and I took over as temporary captain.

Evidently Capt. Lambert thought I'd make captain someday, as he often let me take her in and out of port. In fact, he recommended me for the captain's berth on the Carrollton when he got off; but I didn't get it.

The Carrollton had been built as a coal carrier, with a square stern and two sets of railroad tracks. A string of railroad coal cars would be pushed to the forward cabins and a second string on the second track. They would then alternate opening the cars, so that the boat

120

stayed on a near-even keel. The cars were emptied by knocking open the gates on the bottom of the coal cars.

The ship would back into its slip like a car ferry, so the ship's tracks would line up with the dock's tracks. Her two smokestacks were thwartships, or side by side. She was later used as a scrap iron and pig iron carrier.

She was later sold and her cabins removed so that she could be used as a construction barge in Duluth.

Nineteen-forty-nine was a bad year for me. I spent a little time on four different boats, mostly as 3rd mate: E. G. Mathiott, R. E. Moody, the Carrollton, and back on the Mathiott as 2nd mate, laying up December 15. I was home three different times because of lack of cargo during the summer. And once I had to fire someone in my own family for boozing on the boat.

In most cases the morale of the crew improved with the discharging of someone for insubordination—and we usually held an officers' meeting before discharging anyone.

Again I spent the winter on the car ferries as a relief. From 1950-52 I spent three seasons on the E. G. Mathiott, mostly as 2nd mate, and six weeks as 1st mate.

One time when I was serving with my drinking captain on the self-unloader E. G. Mathiott, we had a load of coal for Midland, Ontario in the Georgian Bay. The captain had never been there before, so he got a pilot to go there with us. I hadn't been there, either, so I stayed in the pilot house and took notes all the way down. It was our first load in the early spring. We arrived at the dock about 5 p.m. The captain, the pilot and a couple of the crew went up the street, partying. The pilot took off. We got unloaded about midnight, and I knew I was going to have a problem awakening the captain. So I took a buddy of his into his room, mostly to witness that I'd tried hard to awaken him. I even got a wet towel and wiped his face; he just cursed and rolled over. So I took the boat out myself.

The captain came up to the pilot house about six hours later, and by that time we were well up through the narrows and in the wide-open Georgian Bay. He was like a wild man, to think the boat had gotten out without his help. If I had let it lay at the dock, I am sure he'd have been fired; but he was far from thinking along those lines.

We were en route to Rogers City for stone, so he said, "When we get to Rogers City, you're fired." Knowing that his 2nd and 3rd mates couldn't load the boat, I told him, "That's okay; when I get her loaded I'll take off."

He came back aboard just before we were loaded. After loading, I got the bill of lading, gave it to him and said, "I am taking off." He answered, "If you do, that's a 'quit.'" I told him, "You fired me." He said, "Oh, no, I didn't. If you get off, you quit." So I stayed. I never, ever quit—although I felt like it a few times.

About five years before that captain was to retire, he was leaving the #3 coal dock in Toledo with a bow thruster and a tug from a straight dock. He crossed the channel and slammed into #2 dock, doing extensive damage. That company told him he had a choice: either retire or they'd fire him. So he retired and got a job piloting on the salt water vessels on the Great Lakes.

CARROLLton

# The Wayne / The Wolverine

*In 1947, at the age of 30, on the recommendation of* my former captain on the International, I took my first captain's job on the steamer Wayne, an excursion steamer operating out of Duluth. She was built in 1923 for the passenger and auto trade between Detroit and Windsor before the Ambassador Bridge was built, and ceased operation there in 1942, after 19 years of service. The Wayne was 135 x 57 x 15. She could carry up to 1,000 passengers, but we had lifesaving gear for only 900, so that was our limit. She was equipped with a 40-foot bar and a dance floor. I was proud of that boat—even though she was like a balloon in the water, and would drift quite a bit in the wind. I learned a lot on her, especially about handling her in the wind. That experience helped me for the rest of my career.

Nick Constans, a marine grocer out of Duluth, bought her and converted her to an excursion boat. She had a 40-foot bar, two dance floors, a series of concessions and slot machines hidden in her wall that they'd pull out on leaving dock. The law made them take the machines out. We had a band, and on nice days that bar would be lined up four-deep

An anchor was stowed on a small shelf on the bow of the boat, and a pelican hook was used to secure it. When there was a need for the anchor, you'd just trip the pelican hook and the anchor would flop into the water. The Coast Guard assumed the boats would have a power winch to hoist the anchor back up, but it was not in writing. Nick had the required anchor but no hoisting winch. This anchor weighed about 1,200 pounds, and attached to it was about 250 feet of three-quarter-inch mooring cable attached to a set of deck bitts. So if you used the anchor, you'd have to get assistance to hoist it.

One Saturday we took off on our first excursion with a full load of 900 persons. No sooner had I cleared the dock when a thick fog set in. I slowly felt my way around the harbor until I came to a flashing white buoy. I got close enough to it to read the number and then positioned myself directly in front of it. Then I plotted a course to my dock, and with the magnetic compass I steered for it. Halfway there I came on a lake freighter anchored, so felt my way around it until I again came to the middle of the boat, backed and filled until I had it right over my stern, then continued on my original course. All the while the bar was busy and the orchestra was playing; the people on board were none the wiser about our problem. We had our three-man deck crew on the bow as lookouts. Luckily we hit the dock right on, and on time for our next revolution. My boss's boss, old Nick, said, "Fine, fine, Captain—we've got another full load for your next run."

There was still dense, dense fog. This was in the middle of September. You had to be on the lake freighters by the 15th of October to be eligible for the 10% fall bonus. I had agreed to a $500-a-month pay, but he asked me to take $350 a month until the end of the year, and he'd made up the difference in one check. I knew how he operated and figured I'd never get my due. I decided that the $1,100 I had coming I could charge to experience. So I said, "Mr. Constans, for my part there won't be another trip in this dense fog. With no radar and no anchor, the risk is too great." He had already sold 900 tickets. So he promised all the ticket holders that their tickets would be good any other time when the weather was clear. Some wanted refunds but he would not return a cent of their money. However, he gave some people as many as five tickets for their one. I left and never heard of him again. Sometime later he died still owing me $1,100.

I quit the Wayne about October 10, 1947, so I could ship on an ore carrier before the middle of October. Then I would be eligible for a fall bonus, if I laid her up. Luckily I shipped 3rd mate on the Wolverine, a grain carrier 414 feet by 48 feet by 28 feet, with wooden hatches and one hatch forward of the pilot house.

The captain and mates slept below the pilot house. The captain had his own toilet facilities, but the mates had to leave the cabin and cross #1 hatch, going down near the crew's quarters to our own toilet and shower. That was always a quick trip as a rule; we never dressed for that trip.

We carried coal from South Chicago to Oak Creek power plant, about eight miles south of Milwaukee. A couple of beautiful, graceful deer used to come down near our ladder, and the crew fed them carrots, potatoes, apples, etc. However, the dock foreman came down and told us not to feed them, and to chase them away, as they might get hurt by our dock cables.

We were going down the Welland Canal en route to Toronto on about the first of July, with a young crew—many of them with firecrackers. The boat was lowered 48 feet in one of the locks. Having to wait about 45 minutes the captain walked back on the starboard side to have lunch. The wheelsman, attending forward winches, had a few firecrackers but was afraid to light them, as the captain might jump him. So I said, "Give me a couple of those crackers." I twisted three together, lit them with Mickey's cigarette, and tossed them into a near-empty cargo hold. These holes are about 100 feet by 45 feet by 28 feet. When the firecracker went off, it echoed, then re-echoed about three times, really making a loud bang.

The captain continued walking aft until he came to the after cabin, then turned and started forward on the port side–the crew's side. The first man he met was the watchman, and he asked him, "Who lit that firecracker." Paul, wanting to protect me, said, "I did, Captain." Then the second man, Mickey, said the same thing.

By that time I was watching Mickey's winches and the captain asked me, "Who lit that firecracker?" Not knowing the other two men had said they did it, and being guilty myself, I said, "I did, Captain." He said, "I'll be damned, it took three men to light one firecracker!

Go around to all the rooms and gather all the firecrackers. Put them on my desk." I took only a handful from each room.

We all got a big laugh out of that ordeal.

~WAYNE ~1000 PASSENGERS
135' x 45' x 15' ~    32 AUTOS

~Wolverine~
413.2' x 48' x 28'-

# The McKee Sons / The Joseph Thompson

*My wife Lou and I were having coffee recently,* and the phone rang: Was I interested in going captain on the McKee Sons? I told him I certainly was, but I'd have to clear it with the union. I called the union, and they said that when I stepped aboard, my pension would stop. I knew that, but then they said, "Here's the sticker—your hospitalization will stop for life." So there went my $350.00-a-day wage. Just couldn't stand that; the McKee Sons' company didn't belong to my union.

McKee Sons is now a barge with a tug inserted in her stern slot, hydraulically jammed, so tug and barge are one continuous unit. As a steamboat the McKee Sons required about 32 men. As a barge set-up, she requires about 18 men. The unit is handled from the pilot house.

The steamer Joseph Thompson was converted to a barge in similar fashion, but her pilot house was cut off, and the tug has an elevated pilot house, about 30 feet above her original one, so she can see over the barge's bow, but is handled from the tug. The difference is due to the Coast Guard's licensing requirements. The McKee Sons, because of being handled from the bow of the barge, requires a full lake master and two full lake mates. The Thompson can get by with tug men, so is a far cheaper operation.

McKee Sons & Tug

# *The G. A. Tomlinson*

*I*was captain on the 532-foot steamer *G. A. Tomlin-*son, a self-unloader, and part of our trade was to service a stone dock in Sarnia near the grain elevators, and also to unload sand at Port Huron's Blue Asphalt dock, just south of where the Sylvania had been docked.

I used to stay about 36 feet off the Canadian shoreline in slack water until I got to the place where I wanted to turn. Then I turned extremely slowly until the current struck my starboard bow, then put her full speed ahead, with hard left wheel. When I was about halfway around, I'd put the wheel hard right to slow her swing. The gyro compass would quickly report her degree clicks—it would sound like a blur—and we'd wind up in the middle of the downbound channel. I used this same maneuver at least 8-10 times.

Once when I was sailing the Tomlinson, we had a load of stone from Marblehead, OH (near Sandusky) bound for Ashtabula. The wind was westerly and building. For guests I had my wife and the 1st mate's wife, who were both in the pilot house to watch us enter Ashtabula.

The wind was behind us, and she rode well, with huge seas passing us. I laid our course for about a mile off Ashtabula, so we'd only roll about a mile going in. About a quarter mile from the harbor light, I headed on the west light with the full gale wind on our starboard side, rolling hard and drifting down. I kept her on the light until I was about a ship's length away. Then I eased her a shade to the left of the light, rolling hard and drifting toward the east light, as we entered the harbor. I had the wheel hard left, to keep the stern from touching the east break wall.

As soon as I entered, I dropped the anchor and full astern, then dropped the second anchor. I finally got her stopped, picked up one anchor and half the chain on the other anchor. So I was dragging one anchor and 200 feet of chain. I squared away and headed for the dock, dragging the anchor.

Everyone had been warned to tie down the furniture, TVs and radios, so we didn't have too much damage. That storm was the topic of conversation for the next few days. Three guys quit, but the women stayed on.

I was loaded, coming down the Detroit River in dense fog on the G. A. Tomlinson when about five boat lengths, or a half mile, from our 90-degree turn the radar corked out. We were approaching the Livingstone Channel, which is like a big 200-foot wide ditch with a rocky bottom. The mate was trying to adjust the set as we approached the turn.

Now, there's a "turn light and horn" at the turn, but it's really a tricky turn even in clear weather. I figured I should be there, so told the wheelsman to start her right. I could feel the butterflies in my stomach. We got about halfway around when I sighted one side bank. We were too close, but all right.

The Tomlinson's career came to an end October 31, 1983, when she was towed from Toledo to Ashtabula for scrapping. She had carried over 20 million tons of cargo, served 78 years and made some $30 million for her owners.

G.A. Tomilson - 1909

# The William J. Delancey

he largest freighter on the Great Lakes, the William J. Delancey, is 1,013.5 feet long, 105 feet wide, and carries approximately 69,000 tons of ore. They load in about six hours and unload in about 13 hours.

She was built in three different shipyards: half of her hull in Toledo, half in Lorain, OH; and all of her cabins in South Chicago. I feel that I played a minor part in her construction.

I was at that time captain on the 600 x 60 steamer Kinsman Independent. We loaded ore in Duluth for South Chicago, and went to the Federal Furnace to unload our ore. We loaded all the Delancey's cabins, filling our cargo hold, and all of the main deck. They were then tack-welded. There was two feet of walking room along the fence to go aft.

We then delivered the cabins to the shipyard in Lorain, where the yard welded the two half-sections of the hull together and attached the cabins to the stern section. My guests for that trip were my wife, Lou, our daughter-in-law Barbara and her son Joshua. We have pictures galore of that ordeal.

On one of my trips, I took John Goudreau and his son Jack aboard from a fish tug at DeTour. We went through the Sault Locks and up the south shore of Lake Superior, and along the Keweenaw waterway through Hancock and Houghton. Jack had gone to college at Houghton (Michigan Technological University), so he especially enjoyed the trip.

One dark, cool November night, as we approached  Standard

Rock in Lake Superior, my watchman noticed a light flashing and called me. I went over to check on it and found it to be a cruiser, about 20 feet long, broken down en route from Isle Royale to Copper Harbor. We lowered three life jackets down to them—a young couple with a daughter about 10. We also lowered three wool blankets and a coil of rope. After securing the cruiser alongside our ship, we towed them slowly towards Copper Harbor. We called the Coast Guard and they towed them into the harbor. Later, the family sent the blankets and life jackets back to us, along with a thank-you card signed by each of them. They also called our company, thanking them for our help.

William & Delancey - 1981
1013' length

# The Wyandotte

One man on my all-time favorite list was Chief Engineer George Hall, who went down with McSorley on the Edmund Fitzgerald. I was captain on the self-unloader Wyandotte and Mr. Hall was her chief. He had never been married, and had bought a lot of stock, so was quite well off. He seldom left the boat, never drank or smoked.

One season they laid up my boat the last of September. I was downhearted about it. A rap came on my office door about 7 p.m. and it was Chief Hall. He said, "I know you have a young family and can't bump back to 1st mate." (Captains were considered executives and not in the union.) He handed me a check for $5,000 to help tide me over until I was working again. He said, "Pay me back any way you wish, with no interest." I said, "Thanks a lot, Chief, but no thanks."

Another time he was my chief and came knocking one night, this time with a $20,000 check, and said, "Take this and buy American Motors stock. It's going to take a huge jump. You can't go wrong, and you can pay me back out of your profit. Again I said, "Thank you, but no thanks." A couple of years later he went down with the Fitzgerald, leaving no relatives. He was a good man.

For years the practice on the lakes was that when the first ship pulled into port in the spring, there would be a greeting by mayor, dock owners and harbor master on shore while they presented the captain with a top hat and a band played. Newspaper and television personnel would be there — a fancy affair.

I was captain on the Wyandotte en route to Windsor, Ontario. A Canadian tanker was following me, and called to ask if he could pass me. I didn't know that he, too, was going to Windsor. I told him, "You can if you're fast enough, but I am not checking." So I called the engineers and told them to open her up full speed. We arrived at Windsor and I noticed the bandstand and a group of people on the dock, all expecting the Canadian to be first.

They tore the bandstand down, and instead of the top hat and overnight suitcase, they gave me the bag and took me up the street for a Reuben sandwich. No television, no dinner with the local dignitaries — just me and the harbormaster and our Reuben sandwiches.

I should have been a Canadian that day.

On the Wyandotte (and also on the G. A. Tomlinson) as captain, I had a basketball backboard installed on the bridge in front of the pilot house, and a 10-foot fence of chicken wire, so we wouldn't lose the balls—but of course, we did. We used to buy the balls three at a time. Our champions varied, but I won once with 21 consecutive shots. The backboard was still on the Wyandotte when they scrapped her.

I was sailing the Wyandotte downbound at Port Huron when a small motorboat pulled up alongside of us. The 2nd assistant engineer came up to the pilot house and said, "That's my wife in that little boat. Can I get off and catch you in Marine City?"

Not wanting to set a precedent, and afraid of a possible mishap, I told him, "I am sorry; if I let you go I'd be reprimanded." So he went back aft and jumped over the stern. She picked him up.

Later when we got to Marine City, he came out in a small boat and yelled, "Lower the ladder!" I told the mate to tell him that he's fired. The company personnel manager and company lawyer met us when we docked in Toledo, but they backed me. I never found out where he went after that.

At one time I was captain on the Wyandotte with a load of molding sand for Windsor, Ontario My wife Lou and I went up the street for our dinner and came back to the ship about 7 p.m. We stood on deck watching the unloading process, with three men in the cargo hold pulling the sand down to the cracked gate. The hydraulically-operated gate, 3 feet square, only opened about four inches because if it opened any wider, the belt would be overrun. The sand running out created a cone-like void.

Suddenly the area mushroomed and filled the void, trappping a worker up to his shoulders. He was at the bottom of the cone with sand running up all around him for about 30 feet. I whistled loudly and the boom operator, at the heel of the 200-foot boom, hit the panic button and stopped everything. I went up and told him what had happened. I worked out a plan: the next time I whistled, he was to open the gate wide below the trapped man and start the belts. My next whistle after that would tell the boom operator to stop everything.

I took a tee-shirt off one of the fellows and tossed it to the trapped man, telling him to cover his head and fasten the shirt tightly around his neck, and then to relax—I was going to bury him, but he'd slip through the gate safely and be all right.

I whistled and the sand came pouring down, burying my crewman. I waited about 10 minutes, and there he came, whistling as he strode down the deck. I asked, "Were you afraid, Frankie?" and he said, "No." "Good," I said, "get back down the hole and help unload." He said, "You don't mean it!" and I said, "Yes, I do; get down there."

A week later I asked him again if he had been afraid, and he said, "I was so nervous, even my feet were sweating!"

About 10 years after I retired, I heard on the scanner that the 1st assistant engineer on the Columbia Star, a thousand-foot freighter, had had a heart attack in the Locks. It was the same Frank, and this time he didn't make it.

We had a severe northwesterly storm in mid-November, so I anchored about a half mile from the beach behind Whitefish Point. We were light and bound for Duluth. A small salt-water boat passed me and anchored about 500 feet off shore. At about 4 a.m., the wind suddenly switched and blew the little salty, which had lost its diesel, sideways onto the beach. Luckily I'd had the engineers keeping the engine warm by turning her over a few times every half hour. We swung around into the wind and I hoisted the anchors and took off for Whitefish Point. My wife was aboard, so I went down to check my quarters—lash the TV, radio and furniture down and tuck Lou in.

Before going down, I'd told the mate not to haul her when he came abreast of the Point, as there would be a strong backlash. I told him I'd be right back. I was just leaving my quarters when the mate hauled her to the right abreast the point. She really rolled, and I scrambled to the pilot house and yelled, "Hard left!" She finally settled down with the wind on her, starboard quarter riding smooth. But the last five hatches broke loose from their fastenings and scattered on deck, with four hatch cover leaves landing in the cargo hold. Luckily the others stayed on deck.

The mate said, "I'll get the whole gang out after breakfast and replace those hatches." I said, "You'll call the whole gang out right now." It was 5 a.m. when all hatches were again secured. A couple had been badly bent. We had shipyard personnel meet us and take the hatch leaves to straighten them out.

The Coast Guard came down and questioned us, and I told them the truth. They accepted my story and never again questioned me. The mate never apologized or said anything in the way of explanation. I never trusted him after that, and asked for a new mate the next season.

Wyandotte -1907

# The William A. Reiss

William A. Reiss - 1925

*I* was captain on the William A. Reiss, and my wife got on for a trip or two in Superior, WI. On the way to the Sault, the cook got violently sick with stomach pains. We put him off at the Sault Locks, and then had no cook. The 2nd cook was a young fellow who had never cooked. So my wife volunteered. She cooked for four days, and in Buffalo we got a new cook. Lou (my wife) did a really good job. At home, we had a family of five, so she just multiplied her recipes by six for our 30-man crew, and most of the time it turned out to be just the right amount. I paid her four days' 1st cook's wages, and explained to the company. They didn't complain.

Once on the Reiss I was following the motor vessel Joseph H. Frantz approaching River Rouge, when the steamer Nicolet gave a security call: "Departing Hanna Furnace on the American side, backing down the river to square away and go into the Windsor fuel dock."

The Frantz called him and said, "We are almost to you. Is it OK to pass you on the right side?" Nicolet said, "OK, keep her coming." So I called the Nicolet and said, "I am close behind the Frantz; OK to keep following him?" He said, "That's OK."

When I got right abreast of him, I made a security call, "Steamer William A. Reiss going into the Windsor fuel dock." Nicolet's captain called and said, "I am going in there to fuel." I told him, "You'll have to wait your turn." He was really upset. I didn't blame him, but we are not out there to win a popularity contest.

# The Kinsman Independent

*I went captain on the Kinsman Independent in the* spring of 1978 and retired off her in the fall of 1985. Three wheelsmen and two watchmen were on the 600-foot lake freighter when I came aboard, and were still there when I left. Captain Routhier of International was on her for 20 straight years, with no summer vacations.

When I was captain on the steamer Kinsman Independent, we were east-bound at White Shoals about 20 miles from the bridge when the watchman, who had been taking down the canvas weather cloth from the bridge in front of the pilot house, got bitten by a bat. I called St. Ignace Coast Guard and asked if they'd take him off at the bridge so that he could go to the hospital and get a shot.

They told me I'd have to get commercial assistance. Knowing there was no commercial assistance at the Straits, and knowing Jimmy Brown had a fish tug, I called Jim. He said he'd be waiting for us. He and his son Jimmy met us off St. Ignace, took my watchman to the doctor and then to the truck stop, where he caught a ride with a trucker who took him right to his door in Duluth. I was really grateful. That same guy today is 1st mate.

One late November I was coming up on Whitefish Point en route to Duluth on the Kinsman Independent. The wind was south-westerly about 40 miles per hour. There were six vessels anchored behind Whitefish. I got the weather report and began to watch the barometer closely, figuring I could get to Keweenaw waterways before the wind went northwesterly. I kept moving, about three miles off the south shore; being in the lee of the land she rode well.

About 4 o'clock the 1st mate came in and said, "You'd better come to the pilot house; she's really howling." I found that the wind had shifted to westerly and had increased quite a bit. The steering pole (a pole about 18 feet long located on the stem, at a 45-degree angle) is rigged up with three lines, one at each side, to keep it from falling towards the water and keep it steady, and a third line strung downward to keep it from rising. So I am sitting, having coffee, and notice that the steering pole is straight upright. The downhaul line had parted. I sent the wheelsman down to assist in grabbing the parted line and tie it together so that the pole was secure. I was afraid the pole was going to come all the way back and slap the pilot house. The men caught the waving line, tied it together, and we were okay again.

The wind was howling so loudly, we had to yell to be heard even in the pilot house. I went into Munising harbor and anchored there for three days. While at anchor I told the mate to check the wheel chains, which were back aft in the fantail and leading from the rudder quadrant to a wooden trough overhead, lined with tin. The trough was about 10 inches wide, with four-inch wooden guide boards on each side. The wheel chains rode in this trough, on to the steam steering engine. A watchman was standing on a six-foot ladder, checking the links. Each link was about five inches long and 3½ inches wide, and the stock of the link about ¾ inches of material.

The mate reached out too far and the ladder gave 'way. He grabbed the trough and at that point, the tin liner protruded about a half inch higher than the wooden guide. He cut the tendons of three fingers. We couldn't raise the Coast Guard, but a fishing boat came out and took him off, and the State Police drove him to the Marquette hospital.

I heard about a year later that he had sued and settled for $96,000. In checking the chains they found one link with only one-quarter of an inch of material left. If that link had parted in the storm, we'd have gotten in the trough of the seas and there's no telling what would have happened. We had just changed those wheel chains two

138

months earlier, but they must have put on a used one.

After that, every boat I'd go on, I'd re-rig the steering pole with ⅛ airplane cable, and never had another line problem.

During a sailboat race from the Sault to Duluth, I overtook a couple of large sailboats beyond Whitefish. In so doing I hauled about a mile to the lee side of them so as not to disturb their wind. When we got back to the Sault, I got a nice thank-you note for being so considerate.

In 1978, most of Lake Superior was frozen, and I was captain on the Kinsman Independent. Until the first part of June, there was still ice from Two Harbors to Duluth. I was eastbound from Duluth and got stuck in the ice off Two Harbors. About four miles to the east of me I saw the Ford steamer Ernest R. Breech coming toward me, so I called and told him I was stuck off Two Harbors, and would he swing close and perhaps break me free. He said, "I am in a track now, and if this track nears you I will." Really, he wasn't in a track, but was going about seven or eight miles an hour, breaking a new trail—so he never came close.

I picked up the A.M. phone and on Channel 51 I broadcast: "This is the Kinsman Independent, eastbound and stuck off Two Harbors, MN. The steamer Ernest R. Breech is coming at me, breaking a new trail. I asked him if he'd come near me so I could break free. He bypassed me and never came close. I'll never buy another Ford product." An A.M. radio phone can be heard all over the lakes, and Channel 51 is an open channel.

About three weeks later I got a letter from the Ford Motor Company saying it was not their policy to bypass customers, and that such an incident would never happen again. They hoped I'd reconsider and continue to buy their products. (Funny thing is, up to that time I had never owned a Ford.)

I retired in 1985. A couple of years later, the company called and asked if I'd help them and take the Kinsman Independent around for about a month; the captain had an eye infection. I caught her in Duluth during the first week of November and got off the first week of December. I had a week of nice weather and three weeks of storms. However, I enjoyed it, and knew most of the crew. I got off in Duluth and drove through Canada, along the north shore of Lake Superior and back to my home in St. Ignace.

*Kinsman Independent - 1923*

# Personal Anecdotes

*fter the lakes sailing season was over, my brother* and I went to Detroit and applied for a delivery car to San Francisco. People in California would buy cars, and Detroit would seek drivers to deliver the cars. We would pay for the gas and oil and keep the receipts, and they'd reimburse us, plus $25.00.

San Francisco's union said we had come down from the lakes to take their jobs. So I asked him, "How about the salt water sailors coming to the lakes?" He said that wasn't their problem. So, we were without jobs, and in a depression.

After a while, our money gave out and we were on our third day without eats. So we saw a sign in St. Catherine's Mission House: "All Welcome." I told my brother that for a meal, I'd give her a try. Jim wouldn't come in, so I went in just before prayer service.

The Sister at St. Catherine's asked if I was baptized. I told her, "No, glory, hallelujah!" So they said a few special prayers and had me strip off all my clothes and put on a hospital gown that had one button on the back of the neck. Then they picked up about five planks from the floor and exposed a 3' x 7' concrete bath tub, three-quarters full of water. All of a sudden, they dunked me, said a few prayers and I was baptized.

I put on my clothes and stood in line with a tin bowl. Finally, my turn came. They had diced boiled turnips—no flavoring, no salt, no pepper, just plain boiled diced turnips. I didn't know afterwards if I was better off or not.

They told me I could stay there 'til I found work. Night came and about 40 of us slept on the floor on papers. We'd work 'til noon, and the rest of the day was ours, so we'd play baseball, softball, basketball, etc. If the weather was bad, we had inside sports—boxing, wrestling, etc.

They had boxing every Friday night, and we'd box just before the big fight we'd box. They picked me for one of the heavyweights. My first bout I hit this kid on the cheekbone and knocked him cold. The coach, a former boxer, said he'd coach me and if I got good, he'd get 80% of my purse, so I signed everything they put in front of me. All I wanted was to put in the winter and get back to Michigan. They kept the money earned until we'd earned enough for our fare home.

One Friday I asked the coach for my $15 before the fight, as my brother had not eaten for a couple of days. I took the $15 out the back door and went straight to the train station. We had about $70 in silver dollars, and we took off for Trout Lake, MI. Those silver dollars were really weighing our pants down. We got to Trout Lake with no boots, no jacket, no gloves or hat, and there was three feet of snow.

Got home and was sure my dad would be glad to see us. But the first thing he said was, "You owe me $9.00 for that C.O.D. bag you sent home." (I'd known we'd soon be broke, and so I sent my clothes home C.O.D. instead of selling them.) Anyway, we made it.

Once I was coming up the Saginaw River on the steamer Crispin Oglebay when a spider bit me on the knee. In a matter of minutes, the knee swelled up to the size of a large melon. I pinned the boat's stem to the river bank, put the engine on slow ahead to keep her there, and called the fire department for a car to take me to a hospital. The mate swung me out onto the deckhand's landing chair. The fire department was there in less than five minutes. I got my shot and pills and returned to the boat.

The winter of '41 and '42 Lou and I met Glen and Joan Shaw of DeTour in Port Huron, MI. We had adjoining apartments on the second story of a house, heated by coal. Glen and I had enrolled in a marine navigation class, and we all had children at home.

It was a severe winter, and neither of us had a car. Our apartments were far from warm. We came home from class one day and found our wives crying. Their stoves had backfired and both ceilings had what looked like three-inch black icicles hanging from them. What a mess we had on our hands. To make matters worse, we were both nearly broke. There were no unemployment checks in those days.

Glen was smart. The first day of our Coast Guard exam, after six weeks of classes, during our lunch break Glen and I discussed the test. We each had been given the same set of questions. When we got back to class I tore up my answers. From then on I was a half day behind Glen. At the end of each day, Glen told me the answers. He got his license in 3½ days, and it took me four days. We both finished in the upper 90s, the top ones in the class.

Glen went 3rd and 2nd mate on the freighter Capt. John Roen, formerly the Hubert Humphrey, which later sank in the Straits of Mackinac. I went 3rd and 2nd mate on the International, which belonged to International Harvester Company.

After six seasons Glen went tugging, and tugged for the rest of his career. We were both made captain at an early age.

One day in late fall, in a blinding snow storm, we were en route to Port Colborne with coal for Toronto and received a radio call from a tug towing a large barge loaded with steel pipe and beams. The captain said, "I've lost my radar and the gyro compass is broken. All I have is a magnetic compass that is 'way off because of my steel cargo.

I got in front of him and headed on to Port Colborne. He followed me and I checked down so he could keep up. We never knew until we got into port that we knew each other. Glen and I have always kept in touch at Christmas, and there's also been an occasional letter about every 10 years or so. Glen's wife Joan and I were both born in Fiborn Quarry, MI0. Now we're all retired; they live in DeTour and we live in St. Ignace.

Years ago as spring approached, I used to get many calls and letters from potential sailors wanting help or advice or seeking sailor jobs. Now, with the lack of Great Lakes freighters and the unions, I seldom get even a call anymore. But along my way, I probably aided over 100 kids.

About five or six kids I assisted wound up being captains. It's really nice to know I helped them get started. Others I helped quit later and didn't even say goodbye.

When I had a hand in picking my crew, I tried always to have a scattered crew, from all over. I tried to steer away from hiring buddies or hometown groups. These often would wind up as agitators and more often bad cliques.

On laying up my first Great Lakes freighter, the Cygnus, in 1937, I joined the union and paid a year's dues in advance so I could work the ocean boats during my winter season.

During the winter months, I planned on winter sailing, so went to San Francisco to ship out. I signed up at the shipping hall and was told I had use of the facilities— pool and ping pong tables, library, outdoor sports.

Later, finding out they were not going to ship me because I was a lake man, I decided to try Los Angeles, so started hitch-hiking. I'd only walked for a couple of hours when a medium-sized truck stopped and the driver asked if I could drive. I showed him my Michigan driver's license and he had me drive the 400 miles to Los Angeles. He had some machines that had to be there, and he was too tired to drive. He bought me two meals and gave me a $20 bill when I got off. I really appreciated that, as I was nearly broke. I put in the winter in Los Angeles and came home in the spring in time for my sailing job.

My wife Lou and our two boys were keeping ship with me one winter in Buffalo. My son Terry was about six or seven years old. The ship, W. C. Richardson, was a crane boat with two cranes on deck, and was used to unload scrap iron and steel. One day I was coming down the deck, and Terry was about 18 feet up on one of the dock cranes.

Just for the hell of it I yelled, "Jump, Terrance," and he did, and landed on my chest, knocking me flat on my back.

Going down the St. Mary's River for a couple of years by the rock cut, I used to see a little boy, about 8 or 9, and his beagle. The boy used to wave a red bandana at me. He always stood in the same spot near two white birch trees. I would blow a salute each time, about 10 minutes before reaching his spot, to let him know I was coming. Then when I saw him I'd blow and wave at him. I always looked forward to seeing that little guy. One afternoon I got there and there was no little boy. His red bandana was tied to the birch tree. Later I found out that his mother, a widow, had died of cancer. The boy was taken to Flint to live with his grandmother. I felt bad about that for a long time afterwards.

I was once shipmates with a small captain on the Lake Michigan car ferries. He was about five-foot-two and his wife was about four-foot-ten. About 15 years before he retired he bought a lot on a hilltop overlooking the town of Frankfort, MI on Lake Michigan. Two years before he retired he built his retirement home, with everything at his wife's height—furniture, restroom fixtures, counter tops, appliances, everything.

In the meantime a family man with five children built a house next door. Not caring for children, the captain's wife refused to live in her brand-new home. So he bought a ready-built home with a couple of acres on both sides of them. It took him over 10 years to sell that little house.

As my family was growing up, we had no winter unemployment checks coming in. Normally I'd get home around the middle of December, and knowing that the steady year-round men would want Christmas and New Year's Day off, I'd call the shore captains of railroad car ferries and tell them I was available for winter relief work.

One year, a steady 1st mate went to marine school in Toledo

and got his master's license before Christmas. Instead of going to the office to record it, he celebrated for two weeks and then went to the office to record his master's license. But I was ahead of him, so he was my mate. He cried all winter that the company was not honoring his seniority.

While my family was growing and I needed winter work, I was never turned down. Later, even though I was 1st mate and captain and didn't really need the work, I never refused their calls when they needed me.

When I do my Christmas cards, I spend at least a half hour on each one, addressing, sketching a little picture and adding a few lines. Then I might get a card from some people signed with just their first names and nothing else—takes them about five to ten seconds.

However, the following letter came one year from a man from Yugoslavia who attended marine school there, got his marine's license and then went into their Navy. After he was discharged, he came to the U.S. and worked as a watchman. One year he was out of work and I gave him a temporary job in June and kept him working until December, relieving the crew. He was about six-foot-four, and powerful. He had one little daughter and greatly appreciated the work I gave him. He never forgot me. Here's what he wrote:

*Dear Captain Ray,*

*I have wanted to write you a letter for a long time, but didn't get the chance. Today when I came home from the boat I got your Christmas card. I was very happy when I got it. This was my biggest present. Thank you for the card.*

*You are retired, you don't sail anymore, but you're always on the lakes and you're a living legend of the Great Lakes. You were the only captain who went on rivers by ship without a bow thruster and without a tug. You were a captain who made big money for the company, and a captain on a boat where there was no sadness. The crew members were happy with you. You were more than a captain on the boat, and I miss you and everyone else who remembers you. Without you no one was happy except the tug company.*

*Sailors are talking about when you came out of the dock gallery without using a tug. I told the captain I have now, about that operation. He said it was impossible. We remember when you came out of port Alpena with no outside help. We also remember coming into Cleveland and going out with no help: no tug, and no bow thruster.*

*You treated us good on the boat. You made big money for the company. Without using tugs, we estimate that you saved around a $1,000,000 a year.*

*Now times are changing. Captains with bow thrusters use tugs for (going) in and out, and use extra fuel for the bow thruster, and don't save much money for the company. But the tug office is happy!*

*Captain Ray McGrath is a living legend and will stay a legend forever on the Great Lakes. One more time, thank you for everything you've done for me, and Happy Holidays to you and the Mrs. Lou McGrath.*

*From Vlado and the Family*
(*Vlado* in Serbo-Croatian is "Walter" in English.

I liked to keep Christmas alive on the boats. Once I bought a piece of marine outside plywood 8 foot x 4 foot x ⅝ inch and cut the outline of a Santa with a bag on his back. I had it all painted and placed it near the top of the smokestack with a couple of floodlights on it. I also had two or three huge Christmas trees on deck with a lot of lights on them. These things I did because we had a crew of mostly young guys. Once when it came time to take everything down, it was mostly my older crew members who would help. I paid them overtime and never celebrated another holiday in that way.

Occasionally I get an unexpected call from out of town or from someone passing through St. Ignace. If I'm not too busy, I always try to meet for coffee. Recently I received a telephone call from a former shipmate. We served together on the steamer International in 1942, and this was the first contact I had with him since that time. It was enjoyable talking with him and reliving some of the incidents that we experienced together.

Recently I received a phone call from the Sault: would I be home tomorrow? "I want to surprise you." He called the next day and asked me to meet him at the "Dockside" for coffee. He turned out to be my deck-watch in 1946 on the Harvester. Forty-nine years ago, and we still recognized each other.

So we spent an hour steam boating. Some time later, I sent him a letter to Sacramento, CA, but didn't know the address so left that line empty. To the left, I wrote "Postmaster, please try to deliver this." My deck-watch got the letter—a PLUS for the post office.

Luckily, I've always been healthy. I sailed for 50 years, from 1935 through 1985, and never had a day off, or a vacation. Most of that time crews did not take vacations. I was only off my boat twice, for family funerals. Today with the unions, officers and crew sail for 60 days and then get off for 30 days with pay. She's a different ball game today. I enjoyed my sailing career and as captain, when all the crew was praying for our last trip to be soon, I'd usually call the office and ask if they couldn't come up with another trip. Often they would, and the crew would be most upset with me.

However, after all those years of sailing, I don't really miss the boats. Most of the 600-foot freighters of my era are now cut up for scrap.

At the time of this writing (summer of 1996) I am 81 years old, a Mackinac County commissioner serving on eight different boards— and my attendance record at meetings is 100%.

# General Shipping Stories

*Keep her on course—*

*Young Captain Ray I. McGrath at the age of 32, when he was on the International*

# The Atlantic Dealer (The Paul H. Carnahan) / The George H. Humphrey / The Smith Lloyd

On July 5, 1945, the 504-foot T-2 salt water tanker Atlantic Dealer was launched. In 1960, she was purchased for conversion to Great Lakes service and towed up the Atlantic coast, through the seaway to Buffalo shipyard, where her bow and stern were sandblasted. Then she was moved to Lorain, OH shipyard for conversion.

A 530-foot midsection, equipped with 21 hatches, was built in Germany and towed 5,250 miles to Lorain. The tow began April 6, 1961, and the section arrived at Lorain June 9, more than 64 days after leaving Hamburg. The tug had run into violent weather and many course changes, and then the captain realized he was running low on fuel. He left a skeleton crew on the tow and cut her loose to drift for three days until he returned fully fueled. The barge was equipped with a radio.

Dry-docked at Lorain, the Atlantic Dealer had its stern cut away and removed and then she was floated out of the drydock and into another dock. The new German-built midsection was floated in and secured to the stern of the tanker. The pilot house stationed amidships was removed and secured to the new midship section, thus making the lake conversion ship, Paul H. Carnahan. Her new size was 707.6 feet by 75 feet by 39.9 feet. The old midsection was taken to Ashtabula, OH for scrapping.

On October 15, 1961, the Carnahan was en route to Superior, WI for iron. She loaded 19,252 tons of ore and departed the same day for Cleveland.

On August 24, 1985, she arrived at Nicholson's in Detroit to

151

await departure to the scrap dock in Taiwan. She and a sister ship, the George M. Humphrey, departed Lorain August 21, 1986, and arrived in Taiwan December 10, 1986. To accommodate the low tow, the Carnahan's fuel tanks were filled; and to further ensure that the towing tug Smith Lloyd would have ample fuel, regardless of the weather, they also put a supply of fuel in her water ballast tanks. When a vessel is loaded, they pump all the water out of the ballast tanks so she'll carry more cargo. When empty, the ship's water ballast tanks are filled so she'll ride deeper and more comfortably.

Atlantic Dealer —
504' x 68.2' x 39.2'

Water Ballast

—Paul H. Carnahan
707.6' x 75' x 39.2'

# The Uri

The Uri was built in 1901, 294 x 62 x 7, with Sulvzer Winterthur machinery: compound diagonal 650 horsepower, and a side-wheeler. She was the oldest of five operating Lucerne paddlers. Held 800 passengers. Rebuilt in 1961 with a hydraulically-operated telescopic funnel (stack) masts and wheelhouse, which could be lowered.

In order to make her able to pass under the new Archeregg Bridge and up the arm of the lake to Alpnachstad, she was converted to oil-firing in 1949. The unusual aluminum awning on the upper deck is to prevent soot from falling on passengers when the funnel is down.

This information was sent me via postcard by Captain William Hoey, Gaelic Tug Company, 24710 E. River Road, Grosse Ile, MI 48138.

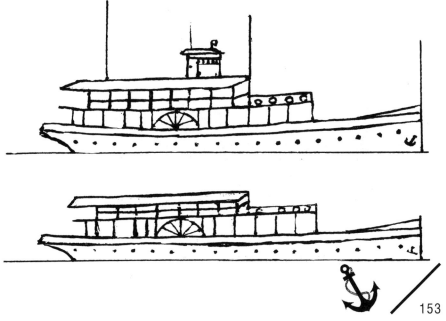

# The Lemoyne

*ames Playfair of Midland, Ontario, launched the* Lemoyne on June 23, 1926. She was the largest ship on the Great Lakes up to that time, and the first vessel with a beam (width) of 70 feet.

She was a beautiful, huge vessel with an extra set of cabins forward. Her very first cargo was 15,415 tons of coal out of Sandusky, OH. Thereafter, she distinguished herself by setting many cargo records. As a result the Lemoyne was chosen to participate in the ceremonies held on August 6, 1932, to mark the official opening of the fourth Welland Canal.

She was reboiled in 1961 and retired in 1968 at 42 years of age. She was the largest laker ever to be scrapped, and the first over 600 feet. Throughout her career she had no major mishaps. She arrived in Santander, Spain in tow of the tug Koral on June 27, 1969.

## LEMOYNE

# The Nevada (The Rogday)

*I*n 1915, the Goodrich Transit Co. built a 222-foot package and passenger steamer, the Nevada. The boat had a full passenger deck, and her single stack was about 30 feet aft of the pilot house. The ship was built for winter use on Lake Michigan, and was so successful that in 1916, the Lake Carriers chartered her to break ice in Whitefish Bay.

Russia was really interested, and bought the boat to break ice in Vladivostok, renaming her the Rogday. Meanwhile, the Russian government was overthrown by the Bolsheviks, and the boat was seized by the American government.

She was purchased by the Muskegon Dock & Fuel Co. and put on the Muskegon-to-Milwaukee run. They renamed her the Nevada, cut her passenger deck off just aft of the stack down to the main cargo deck, and she looked like a pickup truck. She became the first American "roll on-roll off" vessel.

The government requisitioned her in World War II, and she foundered in the North Atlantic December 16, 1943.

*(The Nevada is illustrated on page 112.)*

# *The William G. Mather / Other Museum Ships*

*The beautiful 618-foot Clepeland Cliffs steamer* William G. Mather, a museum in the Cleveland Harbor for the last several years, could not make it financially; it received a letter from the Cleveland Port Authority that it would have to move from its mooring berth by April 30, 1995. The Harbor Heritage Society studied plans with several developers—plans including restaurants and shops in her cargo hold. Then they presented these ideas at Cleveland City Hall. She was given a long-term berth at the East 9th Street pier. I surely hope this beautiful old vessel makes it. Capt. James Doud of St. Ignace, now deceased, once sailed this vessel.

There are several marine museums on the lakes, among them the tanker Meteor, originally the Frank Rockefeller (Superior); the William A. Irvin (Duluth), the Valley Camp (Sault Ste. Marie, MI); the Norgoma (Sault Ste. Marie, Ont.); the Mather (Cleveland); a submarine in Manitowoc, WI; the Willis B. Boyer (Toledo, OH); H.M.C.S.Haida (Toronto, Ont.); the Alexander Henry (Kingston, Ont.); the Huron (Port Huron); the Keewatin (Douglas, MI); the Niagara (Erie, PA); the Norisle (Manitowaning, Ont.); and the Nash (Oswego, NY). *(Some of this information in the second paragraph was taken from **Know Your Ships**, 1996, from the Marine Publishing Company in Sault Ste. Marie, Michigan.)*

# The Helena

The wooden bulk freighter Helena was built in 1885. She was equipped with four masts and two large side-by- side stacks (the normal placing of stacks was tandem, or one ahead of the other). She carried a variety of cargoes.

Her ownership changed in 1911 to the Armour Grain Co. Her new owners made the only drastic change she ever had: They eliminated the two stacks for one large stack, and a grain elevator structure was built on her deck.

. Most of her service was in the Chicago area, but she occasionally made longer trips. One of her longer trips was to Lake Erie, where she was stranded on Sunken Chicken Reef on September 17, 1918. Owners felt it would cost more to put her back in serviceable condition than she was worth. So after 35 years of service she was abandoned.

She was an odd-looking boat, with that deck grain elevator.

"Stmr. Helena"

# The War Fox

*T*he *War Fox* was built for the Cunard Steamship Company of Liverpool, England in 1917. She was requisitioned by the U. S. Shipping Board when the United States entered World War I that spring.

A total of 430 Standard Type vessels were built during the period from 1917 to 1920.

The War Fox escaped war mishaps, and was finally scrapped in Gijon, Spain in August of 1960, after having served for 43 years.

War Fox
251' x 43.5' x 18.5'
1917 - 1960

# The Pere Marquette #3

*here were many Pere Marquette railroad car* ferries, and they usually had a number instead of a name—for instance, Pere Marquette #15, #19 & #20. The Pere Marquette #3 was built in 1887.

Starting from about 1897, the ferries became full sized, around 340 x 58, with four sets of railroad tracks. They had to partially load the tracks to keep her on a near-even keel.

Normal ferries carried about 26 cars, and they all loaded from the stern, so they had to back into their docks. These boats were sturdy, built for year-'round operation. They were all twin-screw vessels.

Their normal run was from Ludington to Milwaukee and Kewaunee.

PERE CHARQUETTE 3 -1887

# The Motor 1

*otor 1 was built by Manitowoc Shipyard in* 1917 for K. Salveson of Oslo, Norway, because the European shipyards were too busy at that time. Her size was 250.5 x 43.5 x 20.4.

She was requisitioned by the United States Shipping Board, and later was sold to Capt. John Roen, who installed two cranes to handle stone and gravel.

She was sold in 1937, and in 1942 was torpedoed by a German submarine; only one life was lost.

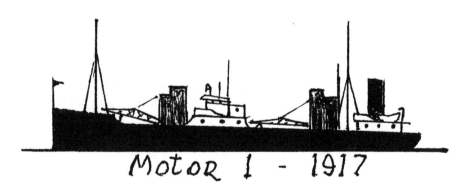

MOTOR 1 - 1917

# The Rockwood

S and dredge *Rockwood* had, in her long life, 10 owners, five re-names, two engines and many captains. She finally wound up with Erie Sand and Gravel Company, and was scrapped in 1963 at Ashtabula, OH.

Rockwood - 1899

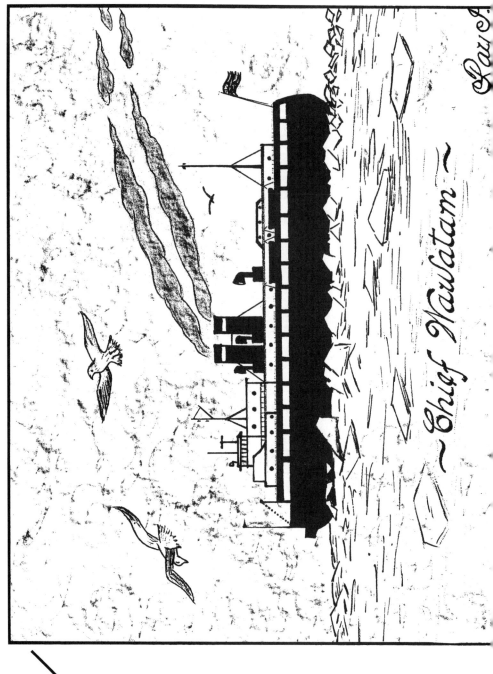

~ Lake Superior ~

Tanker Barge "Cladqco" – 250' x 43' x 26'

# *Lake Customs: Then and Now*

As a rule, when I first went sailing on the ore carriers, on the crew there were: four deckhands; three non-certified deck watches; three watchmen; three wheelsmen; and the mates. Then, along the way, the deck watches were eliminated, and the senior deckhand was promoted to deck watch. He would work days.

However, the custom was that if there was night-docking or working, they'd knock the deckhands and deck watch off early so they could use them for night work and not have to pay overtime. If you did get a few hours of overtime in, they'd knock you off on Sundays to eliminate your overtime. Gradually they knocked deck watches off the crew list altogether. After that, everyone aboard the boat stood four-hour watches except for the captain and the chief—they were on call at any time.

The galley hours were staggered so that at the end of the day, the cook's crew had all accumulated their eight hours. The 2nd cook usually got up at 4 a.m. and did the baking.

At first our working watches were: 6–10; 10–2; 2–6. These were gradually changed to: 8–12; 12–4; and 1st mate's watch, 4–8 a.m. and p.m.

It was always a custom for the captain alone to use the starboard side of the deck. Gradually the mates and the captain all used that side, except in bad weather when everyone chose the safer side.

Anytime the captain came into the pilot house, everyone would stand—and you'd hope never, never to get caught using the captain's chair, which was usually an arm chair on the port side and normally a little higher than the mate's chair. Once I came into the pilot house on the William A. Reiss and the mate never got out of my chair. I asked, "Mate, are you tired?" He answered, "Not really." I said then, "Get your butt out of my chair and keep it out." He said, "Well, I got my master's license last winter." I ended the conversation: "When you start using it, you can use that chair. In the meantime, stay out of it." No more problems with him . . . and the custom carried on.

Before my time there was often a separate table in the dining room for the captain and chief, but in my time the captain just always sat at one end of the table, with the chief at the other. The officers then sat in order of their rank.

And always in the dining room, the captain, chief, three wheelsmen and three oilers all had to have their suit coats on. The captain almost always wore a tie; he and the chief usually wore a uniform cap, also.

In the Steel Trust and a few large fleets, they wore a uniform to meals and for dress.

During the war period I was sworn in as a Coast Guard Auxiliary and given full dress blue uniform, overcoat and lighter-weight gabardine all-weather coat, along with the gold stripes to signify rank. The uniform cap had three tops—navy blue, khaki and white. I had also khaki suit coat and pants, and I usually wore a leather flight jacket and my uniform cap.

Today's dress code on the Great Lakes freighters is strictly casual.

I have never been on a thousand-foot vessel, but Captain Altman, who was on the Edmund Gott, tells me they have eliminated the bell on top of the pilot house. That means that the time is no longer struck. They have also done away with the ringing of the dinner bell, and no longer have the patented deep-sounding rig. Now everything is electronic.

For a while on the thousand-footers they moved the ship's bell forward and used it manually in the fog to warn other ships. Now they've done away with that, too.

Another thing that's gone on today's boats: in former days there was always a speaking tube to the captain's room, with a round, hinged cover and a whistle attached. If I wanted the captain, I'd blow into this two-inch tube and he'd answer. If he wanted us, it would be the same procedure.

Those speaking tubes must have been a carry-over from sailing days and lumber hookers. Another such carry-over would have been a brass message cylinder, about a foot long and three inches in diameter. It had a water-tight screw top, so if something happened you could write your last message and toss it over the side, hoping someone would find it. That practice is long gone now.

All pilot houses used to be equipped with at least one portable bullhorn, used to extend your voice message. Today there's a speaker on top of the pilot house as part of the speaker system.

Also missing now are the portable room fans. Most boats have air conditioning now.

In my day, if you wanted water ballast, you'd call the engineers and give your message: "Start the water ballast in tanks 1, 2, 3, 4 and 5." Then the engineer would watch 6, 7 and 8 to keep his wheel down.

The watchman had a five-foot sounding rod with a rope attached, and would watch the water climb until it got to the required level. Today with the electronic system, everything is programmed; so if you want river ballast, harbor ballast or full ballast for heavy weather, you just need to push the right buttons. The pump will shut off when the desired amount of ballast is reached.

There was always a concern for enough ballast so that the bow and stern thrusters could operate.

On the tug and barge system, if you're towing or in the slot at the stern of the barge, you can drop or raise the anchor with a radio button in the tug's pilot house.

At one time, all boats were equipped with a brass telegraph to the engine room, and also one in the engine room. So if the captain wanted half-speed, he'd ring up half-speed; the engineer would answer with half-speed, which was relayed to the pilot house.

Today all engines are diesel, and the captain controls the engine from the pilot house. This is an excellent system. Today with the satellite navigation system, you can plot your exact position anywhere within inches. This system also enables you to run your true course, regardless of weather changes.

With today's electronic system, your lights go on and off as needed, so there's no chance of forgetting to turn them on. With the modern radars, you can program your courses from Whitefish to Duluth. It'll make true courses good, sound a warning before changing course, and seldom makes a mistake. It will even tell you what time you will reach the next light and how fast you're running.

Today your room temperature is individually-controlled. Your wheelsman programs his course and drinks coffee; he does not have to steer, except in the rivers and harbors.

All of these improvements are fine, but they happened after I retired.

When you're finished unloading and your 250-foot boom is at a 90-degree angle over the side, you just need to hit a button and the boom comes in slowly, synchronizing with the water ballast. (When you swing the boom out, you pump water ballast into the opposite side to keep the ship on an even keel; taking the boom in, you pump water ballast out.) When the boom has returned and is exactly over its resting five-foot saddle, it stops and lowers itself onto the saddle. Then the locking straps are secured and you can take off.

The average speed of a 600-foot boat was about 12 miles per hour. Now the twin-screw thousand-footers go about 17 miles per hour.

167

We used to carry about 14,000 tons of ore. Today the big boats carry about 65,000 tons. And everyone lives aft, with the forward cabins gone.

~The INTERNATIONAL ~

Crispin Oglebay - 1908

# ☞he ᴄ𝒜nchor

*ost captains seem hesitant to use the anchor. I* started out on smaller boats without much water ballast. Draft increases with increased water ballast, as your ship is deeper in the water and easier to control; wind has less effect when you're deeper. I needed all the help I could get.

Often when the wind was strong and I was coming into a dock too quickly, I'd use two anchors. I learned that when using two anchors, you never have as long an anchor chain lead on the second anchor, and always hoist the second anchor first because there's always a chance that the anchors may cross.

I've been on boats with crossed anchors, and had to spend hours trying to un-cross and hoist them. I've also had a situation where we couldn't untangle them and had to hoist both crossed anchors as far as we could, and then have a tug and barge or raft with a welder and burner's torch aboard. We had to get those anchors powered down on the raft, burn one line and free the chain, then weld the links together again. Each anchor weighs about 3,500 pounds; weight depending on the size of the boat, and size of the chain-links depending on the anchor weight. An average 600-foot boat would have an anchor weighing about 3,500 pounds, and each link of the anchor chain would be about 10 inches long and would weigh about 40 pounds. The more anchor chain lead you have, the more chance your anchors will cross, because a drifting ship would have to drag all that chain.

As a rule, when you hoist your anchor with a steam windlass or engine, the anchor holds and you're shorting up your chain and dragging your boat over the anchor, where it'll be hoisted far more easily.

The reason for this long-winded explanation is that I am sure many of the readers of this book will not be boat people. From the following sketches, we'll assume the boat is 500 x 50 x 30 and also realize that a long anchor lead will hold the boat better than a short lead.

Figure #1: If your boat is drifting sideways, always drop the anchor from the lee side. The lee is the protected side. In figure 1 the chain anchor will drop straight down and under the ship, securing much faster.

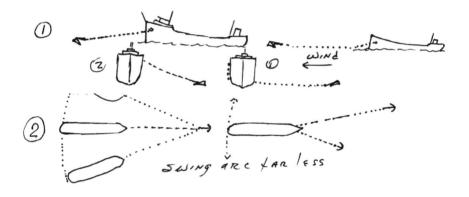

Figure #2: Your chain is pointing up and won't be too effective. Often when you're anchoring your ship with only one anchor, the ship can move in a large arc. With two anchors it will often lie more still. Most anchor chains are color-coded red/white/blue, so you can estimate the amount of chain you have out. Starting at 150 feet—one red link; 200 feet—two red links; 300—feet three red links, 400 feet—one white; 500 feet—two white; 600 feet—three white; 700 feet—one blue; etc. If you're downbound in a river and have to anchor, and happen to have a stern anchor, stop your boat and use your stern anchor. The current will hold your boat in the down direction.

Figure #3: When leaving a dock, back your boat as fast as you can. Then, nearing the end of the dock, shut your engine off. The boat will straighten itself on the dock, and then have ⅓ right rudder, as the boat tends to go in the direction the rudder is pointing, or may go straight back but just coast. Anytime you use your engine on backup, the stern will always back to port (left). When you've gone back far enough, hard left rudder and full ahead on the engine. When she loses sternway and starts ahead, drop starboard anchor and go slow speed on the engine. At slow speed the anchor will hold and you can come left to your desired direction. Hoist the anchor and take off. Starboard anchor will lead under the ship and give you better holding power.

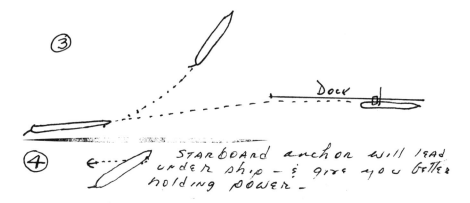

When you're in a port with a turn basin—such as Indiana Harbor, South Chicago, Buffalo, or Munising—and you have no bow thruster, go slowly to the extreme end of the turn basin, but drop your opposite anchor before crossing the basin. Have your brake on the anchor windlass, so your chain plays out as you proceed. Near the far end of the turn basin, put the brake on the windlass, hard left wheel, and slowly enter the basin. Your anchor will hold.

With a mate at the stern to keep you informed on stern position, keep the stern in the middle of the river and have the mate hoist the anchor. The anchor windlass will pull the bow to anchor position.

Hoist the anchor and take off.

Always check the chart for submerged pipelines and cable crossings when going to anchor. Never drag an anchor through a bridge area, as there's nearly always buried cable there. When entering ports or anchor areas, always lower both anchors about six feet to be sure they're free to go and not frozen up. See sketch:

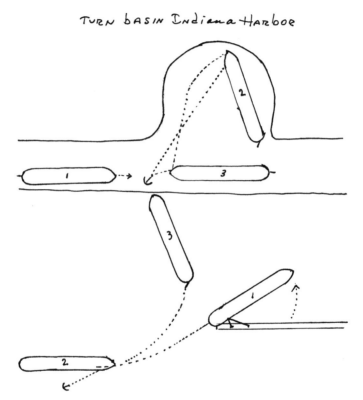

I used this method for three consecutive stone trips into Indiana Harbor on the James E. Ferris, and the company was so impressed they raised my pay class from 2nd to 1st.

Continuing are some anchor diagrams I have drawn to illustrate some principles for their use:

172

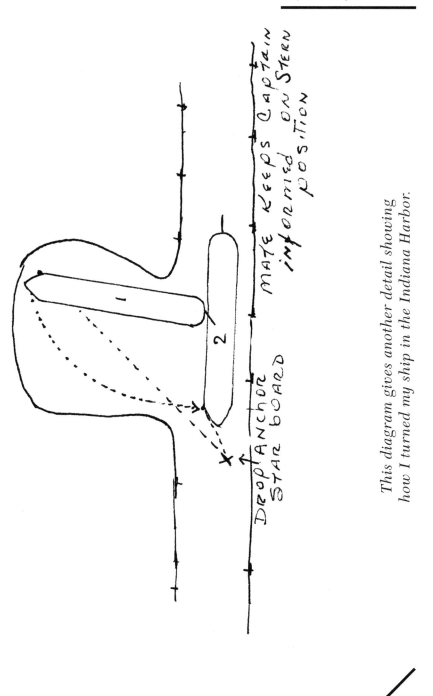

*This diagram gives another detail showing
how I turned my ship in the Indiana Harbor.*

173

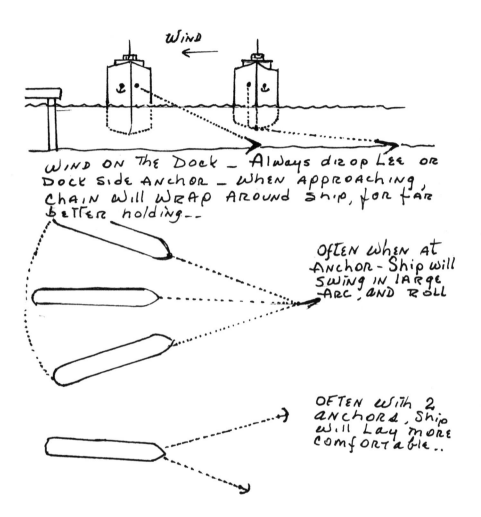

WIND

WIND ON THE DOCK — Always drop Lee or Dock side Anchor — When approaching, chain will wrap around ship, for far better holding——

OFTEN when at Anchor — Ship will swing in large Arc, and Roll

OFTEN with 2 anchors, Ship will Lay more comfortable..

*These are illustrations of how*
*to use the anchor in wind.*

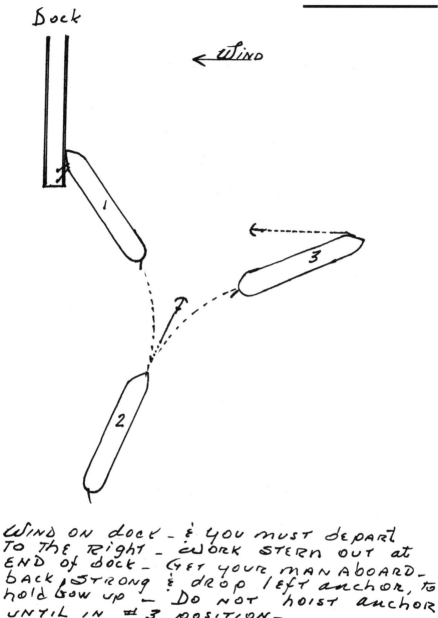

Dock

←Wind

1

3

2

WIND ON dock — & you must depart
to the right — work stern out at
end of dock — Get your man aboard —
back strong & drop left anchor, to
hold bow up — Do not hoist anchor
until in #3 position —

*...And more illustrations of how
to use the anchor in wind.*

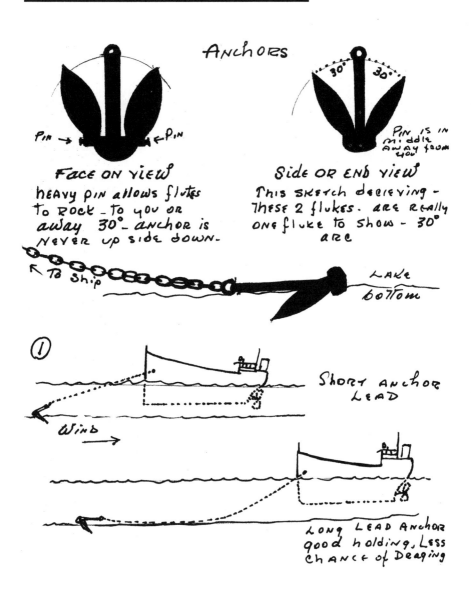

These are illustrations of
anchors and how to use them.

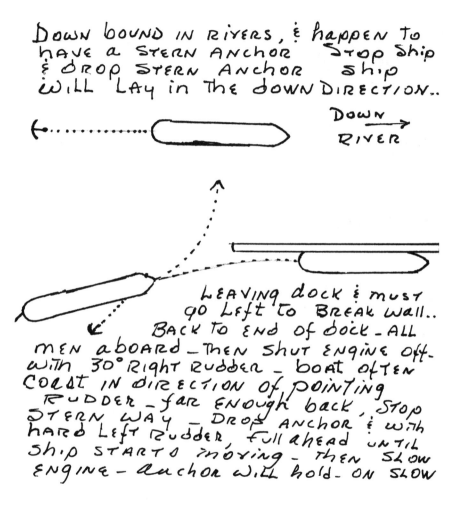

Down bound in rivers, & happen to have a stern anchor. Stop ship & drop stern anchor. ship will lay in the down direction..

Down ──→ River

Leaving dock & must go left to break wall.. Back to end of dock _ all men aboard _ then shut engine off _ with 30° right rudder _ boat often coast in direction of pointing rudder _ far enough back, stop stern way _ drop anchor & with hard left rudder, full ahead until ship starts moving _ then slow engine _ anchor will hold _ on slow

*These drawings show how you can use the anchor to help you lie still or turn.*

Dock Bollard
3' x 1' x 4"EARS

Dock cleat
20" x 5" x 4" MATER
ial

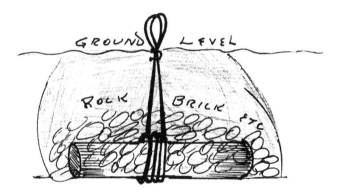

Winter dead man - 6' RAIL ROAD TIRE
Buried 6' deep - WRAPPED with ¾" Cable
use with Steel Shackle - OR Toggle

*These are illustrations of dock fastenings*
*for your boat.*

Often when anchoring in shoal water or making docks, when the water shoals at the inner end of the dock, ships will drop their anchors and then run up onto it and punch a hole in the bow. Once I punched a hole in the bow of my boat while making the Marblehead, OH stone dock.

My ship tore into a three-foot x one-foot steel tie-up dock bollard, which went into the water and was never recovered. A bollard is used to fasten the ship's cables. There had never been a warning issued about the bollard. I made an approach to the dock in a bad storm. The rip occurred about 12 feet off the dock, and I never knew about the hole until the next morning when we found the torn peak half full of water.

Rivers are like deep ditches. A captain departing St. Clair in a dense fog, not wanting to run aground, dropped his anchor and then picked it up, so it was just touching the bottom. He figured that if he went out of the channel, the anchor would grab and he could pull himself free. But if he pulled the anchor up out of the channel, he would punch himself. He did that only once.

# Ferries and Barges

Occasionally I see the once-proud ice-breaking railroad car ferry Chief Wawatam, now a barge for the Purvis Canadian tug Company of Sault, Ontario. I worked hard trying to get her placed just west of the Mackinac Bridge, in a ditch right near the shore and pointing west, as a museum and tribute to the very successful ice-crushing car ferry.

I worked on the railroad car ferries during the winter months before they had gyro compasses (gyros are not affected by magnetic fields like flat cars loaded with steel pipes). We'd load and depart, and then as we reached the lake, the captain would send the mate up the forward spar to the crow's nest. There was a compass in the nest and a speaking tube that was connected to the pilot house. We'd then give the pilot house our compass reading and he'd allow the difference between compasses to his courses, the spar compass being about 45 feet higher than the pilot house compass. In zero weather, the two-inch ladder rungs were about four inches in diameter, so you had to hug them to climb up and down the spar ladder. I never liked that job, but never fell. After gyro compasses were used, that job was eliminated.

After I completed high school in 1935, I secured a job with the state ferries doing some relief work. I worked wherever I was needed until 1938. Then, wanting to become an officer, I quit and got a job on the Great Lakes ore carrier Cygnus. Up to that time I had worked on the Straits ferries St. Ignace, Mackinac City, Straits of Mackinac, City of Cheboygan, City of Petoskey and City of Munising.

Those last three ferries carried about 120 autos each. The Mackinac auto bridge was completed in 1957, so the ferries were no longer needed.

In 1935, my first job was as deckhand on the Michigan State ferry St. Ignace. Her chief engineer was my neighbor, Leo Fogelsonger. Years later I was best man at his son John's wedding, and even later was godfather at John's daughter Debbie's baptism. I gave her a small silver rosary. When she was four years old, and playing behind a customer's car at her grandmother's store, the customer backed over Debbie, killing her. In her casket she had the rosary, wrapped around her hands.

Years later, John was 2nd mate on the Carl D. Bradley. John's wife had a new baby, so I sent her a baby scale. John was upbound off Milwaukee and I was downbound. We had a northwest gale. John called to thank me for the baby scale. It was near the end of the season, so I asked John if he was going into Manitowoc to lay up. "No," he said, "the yard is busy, so we're going to make one more trip." As I was entering Chicago, the mate told me he'd just heard the Bradley had touched Boulder Reef, was breaking up and sinking fast. Only 2 of her 36-man crew were saved — 1st Mate Fleming and Deckwatch Maze.

Deckwatch Maze quit sailing and got a job in the stone quarry. Mate Fleming, who built a new home outside Rogers City, was promoted to captain in the spring, but after a couple of months asked the company for a mate's job. He couldn't take the stress and strain of the captain's job. He retired a couple of years later and started to write a book, but died before the book was finished. His black hair had turned snow-white.

John's widow, Mary, asked Mate Fleming where John was the last time he saw him. Fleming told her John had just been on his way aft for his supper, and was at #2 hatch, over the crock or just past it.

In the middle 50s, the Ann Arbor car ferries were painting their hulls in the spring. My brother had just put a new film in his camera. Looking out the porthole, he noticed that the adjoining ferry was preparing to lower a stage plank to paint the bow. So he took a picture as they were first lowering the plank, and then another as the plank was placed and tied in place. Then, as the second man got on his end of the plank, my brother took a third picture.

Then the knot slipped, and one man fell into the water, and another climbed aboard. My brother took a series of pictures, as the man was in the water. The nearby Coast Guard station was notified. The man drowned before help could get to him.

Sometime later, my brother brought the film to the local drug store to get it developed. The clerk told him that in about a week the photos would be back. About eight days later, he went to get his pictures and the same clerk told him, "You didn't leave any film here." My brother said, "I surely did, and I gave them to you." The guy said, "Sorry, I never saw you before." I am sure he sold them to the railroad company that owned the ferries.

Out of St. Ignace we have three passenger ferry boat companies. Occasionally I'll park on the docks and watch these ferry boat captains land and depart. I've got to commend them—they really do a splendid job. I've yet to see one of these ferries bounce off the dock. They slide up to the dock as if they had wheels.

The small wooden passenger and auto carrier Ariel was purchased to serve the public in transit between St. Ignace and Mackinaw City. The vessel formerly ran between Detroit and Windsor from 1881 to 1922. She was sheathed with iron to her hull to help her handle any ice problems.

She ran for Michigan State Ferry Service for five years, from 1922 to 1926. When the state's business began growing rapidly, she was replaced by larger vessels—the Mackinaw City, the St. Ignace, and the Straits of Mackinac. These ferries were around 175 feet in length and 45 feet wide, and served well until 1937, when they were helped with the addition of the City of Cheboygan, the City of

Munising, the City of Petoskey, and finally the diesel-powered Vacationland, bringing the total to seven ferries. The Vacationland was a double-ender, meaning that she had engines on both ends and never had to turn around.

These ferries ran until the Mackinac Bridge was opened in 1957. The ferry service meant an awful lot to the economy of the Straits area. However, now the Mackinac Bridge is also helping our economy.

The year 1947 was a tough year for me. I worked only three months on the freighters—June, July and August—and had two sons to support. So I got a mate's relief job on the Ann Arbor car ferries, out of Frankfort, MI. I worked there until April, when I went back on the lake freighters.

Thereafter I worked on the car ferries winters, until they folded up in 1982, and worked mostly as captain for the last 15 years. They always had a job for me when I needed work, so I never refused work when they needed me. My favorite car ferry was the motor vessel Arthur K. Atkinson. I was captain on her many, many times.

In 1978, Lake Michigan froze over completely, but we never stopped running, although we often got stuck. We helped each other. The ferries were twin screw, fast, and fun to handle.

I remember the winter when I was captain on the twin-screw railroad car ferry City of Milwaukee. Lake Michigan was frozen all the way across; the ice didn't stop us, but we bucked it all winter.

Once I got stuck between Frankfort's piers for three days, waiting for the wind to shift. We put a boarding ladder down and let the people walk about a quarter mile to the dock. The passengers were really nice and waved goodbye as they departed. Our crew helped with their baggage. We even had a sleigh full of groceries delivered while we were stuck there. We had oil fuel at our docks, so always had a full bunker before departing.

Another time I was on a car ferry and taking a walk in Manitowoc, when a fellow in an old car, with his family of four, stopped me and asked if there was any way he could work his way across the lake. He said he had lost his Wisconsin job, and was returning to his folks in Grand Haven flat broke.

He really looked pathetic. It was a cold night, and I knew what it was to be broke. So I went to the Purser and said, "Douglas, if you let that poor family across free, I'll give you a trip off—but keep it on the 'Q.T.'" He said, "You're on." I went back and told the family to get in line and come aboard. I also gave them a lunch on the way across the lake.

About three months later, the man sent me a thank-you note and a picture of his new baby. I really felt good about that, having come from a large family myself.

In the 60s I was mate on the car ferry City of Green Bay during the winter. I came into the captain's quarters one cold, cold day, and the 70-year-old captain was sitting in the center of the office with a fire going in his waste paper basket. He said, "It's cold in here." I called the office and told them. When we arrived in Frankfort, MI., they had a new captain waiting. I never saw the old captain after that. I heard he was in a rest home. Really a nice old guy.

Oddly, the new captain stayed only a couple of weeks. We got loaded one night about 10 p.m. and there was no captain. We waited about an hour, and he and a girlfriend came down to the boat. He came aboard, got his license and clothes, and took off. I called the Superintendent and he said, "You're the captain. Get going." So I had the job until spring. Sure liked her—twin screw and lots of power.

*The Detroit News* came out with a full-page story and picture of the Coast Guard cutter Escanaba breaking ice and escorting eight lake freighters westbound through the Straits, but there was no picture or mention of the car ferry Chief Wawatam, ahead of the Escanaba, breaking the original track.

One winter I worked mostly on the Chief Wawatam and the

Sainte Marie railroad car ferries across the Straits of Mackinac. We carried mostly railroad boxcars and a few autos. The state ferries did not run during the winter months, as winter traffic was almost nil; they were overhauled during the winter.

The Wawatam could carry about 26 boxcars and 516 passengers. She was 338.8 x 62 x 25. The Sainte Marie was 250 x 62 x 25; she'd carry about 16 boxcars and 400 passengers, but being the shorter vessel she was a better boat in icy conditions. These ferries had twin screws aft and a single screw (propeller) forward. The forward screw was like a club wheel, not meant for propelling, but to suck the water from under the ice in front, so the ice would break up more easily. The Sainte Marie was a backup boat for the Chief, but the Chief was so reliable she seldom broke down, so the Sainte Marie had a pretty idle life. She was cut for scrap in Ashtabula, OH and the Chief Wawatam was sold to Purvis Tug Company in Sault Ste. Marie, Ontario, where the cabins and engine were removed, a "V" slot was cut in the stern for a tug's bow, and she is now used as a tug and barge combination.

Once I had a 1st mate who was raised on a reservation in Bemidji, MN He also attended a Native American college. I asked him what "Wawatam" meant in his tribe, and he said "wa" meant big and "tam" meant canoe, so Wawatam meant "big, big canoe" in his tribe. . .which is far more logical than a lot of local translations I've heard.

While working on the Chief Wawatam, a watchman who was going to do a little building, took lumber off the railroad flat car when the wind was easterly. He'd shove the lumber out the porthole and after he was off the boat he'd run along the shoreline with his truck and pick up the lumber. I don't think he was ever caught. (Easterly winds would blow the lumber ashore.)

I was 1st mate on the railroad car ferry City of Green Bay, going into Manistique, and I recall the captain telling me that when entering that harbor, always come on due north—never, ever to the right of north. So along my way, I always did that.

Some time later I was telling one of the skippers that advice. He said, "That old captain doesn't even know his own name anymore; don't pay any attention to him." But I did. A month later that same winter, that unbelieving captain took the bottom out of his ferry while coming into that harbor to the right of north. The Coast Guard found him to be lying at the inquest. In the end, the company fired him.

Another time I was captain on the car ferry City of Milwaukee, approaching Frankfort. I noticed the motor vessel car ferry Viking stuck right at the entrance to the harbor, so I called him and he asked me to try to break him loose. The bow of the Viking seemed to be raised up about five or six feet in the thickened ice, and the wind was brisk. So I turned around and was backing toward him, heading on his pilot house because of the wind. Before I knew it I was nearly up to him. So I put her full ahead on both engines to wash the ice away from his stern and to slow myself down. He was backing strong. My stern hit his stern about two feet from the end of his boat and gave him a great jar; he backed right out into the lake about a mile, came racing back and plowed right into the harbor with me about 200 feet behind.

I was captain on the twin screw diesel railroad car ferry in a northwest gale, en route from Frankfort, MI to Manitowoc, WI when the steering engine quit on us. So I put the starboard engine on ¾ speed ahead and left it there on the port engine. (We used the engines to steer her if I wanted to go right a bit; we'd go full ahead on port engine if we wanted to go left a little. We'd slack off on the port engine after about a half hour.)

The wheelsman got on to that and steered her with the engine to within two degrees in the storm. To be extra cautious, I called for a tug to pick us up outside the breakwall and take us to the dock, but he would not come outside the breakwall, so we had to come in and dock her by ourselves.

After completion of the Mackinac Bridge, the state ferries were abandoned and the sailors had to seek boats elsewhere. One of our captains got a job as captain on a towing tug out of Chicago. His first tow was a large barge loaded with large construction pipe. On entering Milwaukee, he checked the tug down, but forgot about the barge following him; it rammed the tug and nearly sank her.

He was on the next Greyhound for St. Ignace.

Luckily, while I was working on the totally pure-white Michigan State Ferries, they never had a mishap. That was 1935-37, before radar. But I do remember that when crossing in dense fog, the captains used to have two or three of us on the bow, and one of us on top of the pilot house listening for fog horns and trying to spot oncoming ferries. Being white and in dense fog, they were really tough to spot. The Wawatam, being black, was much easier to see.

I was deckhand on the Straits car ferries during hunting season. A large, black Lincoln was parked right at the ramp and would be the first car off. As we approached St. Ignace, the driver handed the watchman a fifth of scotch and said, "Have a drink, Sailor." The watchman stuck the bottle in his coveralls and under his belt. He let the ramp down and waved for the Lincoln to move on out. The driver said, "My bottle." The watchman said, "You're holding up traffic; move on out." So he lost his bottle.

I sailed 40 winters on car ferries, the last 14 years as captain. The ferries were well-built, sturdy boats, all twin screw and loaded from the stern.

Western Star - 1952

# *Bow Thrusters and Tugs*

*Y*ears ago before ships were equipped with marine radio telephones, each fleet company had a certain signal, and each ship in its fleet had a separate signal. So passing through the Straits, which was always a reporting station, you'd first blow your fleet signal, then follow with your boat's signal. So the total time to blow signals could be long, with each blast being about two seconds apart, and about five seconds between fleet whistle and boat signal.

Today that system is obsolete. All ships report positions with radio phones . With the addition of bow and stern thrusters, the use of harbor tugs is much less. A bow thruster is a propeller approximately six feet in diameter, placed in the center of a horizontal cylinder pipe, parallel with the water's surface approximately at the 13-foot draft mark near the stem. It controls the bow or stern to the right or left. It is controlled by the pilot house.

With the use of these thrusters, you easily handle either end of the ship, or both ends at the same time, making your docking easy.

My ship, the Wyandotte, was laid up temporarily with boiler problems, so I was called to be relief captain on the Crispin Oglebay, which was unloading stone at Upper Republic, Cleveland. I boarded her about 7 p.m.; she was due out around midnight, so I went to bed.

The mate called me and said, "We'll be unloaded in half an hour, and I've got two tugs ordered for you." She had a bow thruster, so I asked, "Why two tugs?" He said, "That was Capt. Joe's order." I said, "Capt. McGrath's orders are: one tug." So I came out stern first with one tug.

When I was selected to go permanent captain on the steamer Ben E. Tate, she was in dry dock in Lorain, OH and was to be floated about 2 p.m. So the mate came to my room and said, "Two tugs, Captain?" I said, "No, we'll try her by ourselves." After a full ballast, we backed out, went up the river to the steel mill's turn basin, turned on an anchor and came out—no problem.

Another time I was captain on the steamer Ben Morrel, coming out of Cleveland stern first with a stern tug. We got about halfway out and the tug called and said, "We'll tie up here for an hour; we're going to the office to change crews." I told him, "If you leave me now, don't come back." So I continued, stern first, no tug—but I did have a bow thruster.

I was on the James E. Ferris and got unloaded at Buffalo grain elevator. I called for a tug, and the tug office said, "There's a boat aground at Tonawanda in the Black Rock Canal. Expect about a 10- to 12-hour delay. They have all six tugs on her." I went up to the turning basin, turned on an anchor, and continued on my way. The next day Mr. Steinbrenner called and said, "I have nothing for you; I just wanted to thank you for the extra effort in getting that boat out of Buffalo."

Yet another time the captain and chief were getting only 2nd class wages because the boat was only 450 feet long. I had three cargoes of stone out of Port Inland for Indiana Harbor. I delivered all three and turned in the turn basin with no tug. The next time I talked to the office, I was told, "As of the first on the month, you're on 1st class wages, but don't tell the chief; he stays on 2nd class."

Then there was the time I was unloaded in Buffalo, called the tug office and was told there would be about a six-hour wait: "Too much weather; the seas are coming right over the breakwall." I didn't believe him, as we had little wind where we were. So I took off, turned at the turn basin with no tug and no bow thruster. When we got to the breakwall, there was a one- or two-foot sea. That was the first time I had turned a 600-foot boat. Because I had done it, the rest of the fleet was also asked to do it; so I ended up on the bottom of the totem pole in terms of popularity!

One time I was scheduled to go to Duluth and load grain for Oswego, NY and was just about to depart from Buffalo when the foreman yelled, "Call the office!" I went ashore and was told, "We just got word, the dock wants a boat with hatches 12 feet apart." Mine were 24 feet apart, so would carry a little less. I was asked if I could go up to Alpena to load cement clinkers for Superior. I had previously checked the harbor really well, with dividers, so I knew I could turn. I told him yes, and he told me to go ahead, and also to fuel there. No previous ship had ever turned in that harbor without bow-thruster or tug assistance. We had no bow thruster and no tug available. After we were loaded, it took me nearly an hour to turn, but I made it. Again I was unpopular, as that began a new business: other captains also had to go in without assistance.

As a rule, I had the lowest tug bill in the fleet. In my time, one tug was $5,000 and two were $10,000 (no break for using a second tug). Buffalo was usually one tug in and two out, $15,000 a trip.

Not long ago the motor vessel Indiana Harbor left Sturgeon Bay shipyard at 9:30 p.m. en route to Duluth. At 2:30 a.m. she ran full speed, 17 miles per hour, smack into Lansing Shoal Light near Manistique. She had a hole in her bow 60 feet x 40 feet, and took 400 feet of the bottom out of her. It cost approximately $70,000,000 to construct the boat, and the estimate for repairs was up to $5,000,000.

The Indiana Harbor had the very latest of navigational equipment, but you've got to be awake to use it. She was able to back off and limp into upper Green Bay shelter, then on to the Sturgeon Bay shipyard for repair. The only good thing about the mishap was that the Sturgeon Bay shipyard would do the repair work.

190

In back of the pilot house on all newer boats is a chart room with desk chairs, a rest cot, coffee, etc. It is guessed that the mate and wheelsman went back for coffee, fell asleep and the boat was left on automatic . . . kept on going 'til she plowed right into the light.

Nearly the same thing happened some time ago to the Kinsman Independent. She rammed head on onto Isle Royale going 14 miles per hour, 24 miles to the west of her charted course—in clear visibility. Again, I guess, no one was in the pilot house. Her damage was $1,500,000.

## "Tug Favorite"

The tug Favorite, 180.7 x 43 x 20.6, was launched February 2, 1907, in Buffalo, NY for the Great Lakes Towing Company of Cleveland. She was the largest self-propelled vessel built for salvage and rescue work on the Great Lakes.

She was stationed at St. Ignace for some time under the command of Capt. Alex Cunning. During the next 10 years she was involved in many notable salvage jobs. On May 29, 1909, the car ferry Ann Arbor #4 capsized at her dock at Manistique, MI. It took a month to right her. Later she was the City of Cheboygan Michigan State Ferry, and I was watchman on her under Captain Andy Coleman.

In July of 1915, the Favorite was involved in the grim task of raising the passenger steamer Eastland after she rolled over in the Chicago River, taking 835 lives with her. On November 23, 1917, the Favorite was taken over by the Navy. On her way out of the lakes, she assisted in freeing the vessels Colorus and George N. Orr, which were aground on Prince Edward Island.

~ EastLand ~
265 x 38.5 x 19.5   Passengers 2500

Until March of 1918, she was involved in breaking ice off the coast of Maine. In August of 1918, she arrived in Brest, France, and salvaged sunken vessels for a year in that area before returning to New York.

In 1940, the Navy sent her to the Panama Canal, where she remained until 1948. Her next home was Lima, Peru, for the Peruvian Navy as a submarine rescue vessel. After 51 years, she was scrapped. Her gross tonnage was 1,223.

Years ago when we'd go to Oswego, NY, we'd often see canal boats with two or more barges ahead of them loaded with grain. On top of the house we'd see chickens and geese penned up, and occasionally a pig or two. Canalers were usually operated by one family.

Before Great Lakes tugs were dieselized, that smoke was terrible, especially in a slight head wind. The harder that tug would work, the blacker and denser that smoke would be—and fire-red sparks would shoot up from her stack. It was nice after the diesels were installed. Today, with bow thrusters, the tugs are no longer essential. In fact, some of the thousand-footers also have stern thrusters.

A veteran salt water captain made a trip on the Great Lakes and got violently seasick. Until the episode, he had always considered the Great Lakes to be a series of puddles. He later claimed he had become ill because the lake waves were much faster and choppier. He was used to the long, slow swells on the ocean.

Compared with ocean shipping, the whole lake industry is much faster. Turn around time on the lakes is faster, and only a fraction of an ocean ship's time. Each trip for a lake ship calls for continuous navigating skills. A lake captain is his own pilot, whereas on the ocean a special pilot comes aboard the vessel when she nears a port.

Also, you note the differences in the makeup of the crews. After each trip the ocean crew is paid off, so they must then seek another ship. The lakes crews are not a transient lot. A lake sailor boards his vessel in April and is paid off in December, with 3½ to 4 months off-time during the winter. And most often, he goes back to the same ship in the spring.

~ City of Milwaukee 1931 ~

My favorite car-ferry - built 1931 - and it's idle in Frankfort Mich. harbor. since 1982

193

# IV

# *Personal Stories*

*Keep the wind on your back—*

*The 30-year-old Ray I McGrath looked
perfectly at home on the boat in 1945.*

# Family & School Tales

My dad's parents were both born in Ireland and married there. His mother's name was Bridget Sharkey, and his dad's was James McGraw. Somewhere along the way, the name wound up "McGrath," as did the last name of his brothers John, Nick and Mike. They were all well over six feet tall, which was really tall in those days. The four brothers all settled in St. Ignace, MI.

My mother's parents were both born in a little town outside of Helsinki, Finland, and my mother was also born there. Her dad, Mr. Weeda (I never knew his first name), came over first and found work in the lumber camps around Newberry, where he became foreman and bought a house in Dollarville. He then sent for his wife and daughter, Ina (my mother). She remembered later that she was about eight years old when she and her mom boarded the passenger boat for the United States. She recalled the whales swimming alongside the boat and spurting water into the air.

There were three boys and one girl in my mother's family and she outlived them all. There were seven children in my dad's family, and he outlived all of them, also. He was 95 and my mother was 98 when they died. My dad, Owen, was the only member of his family who remained in St. Ignace.

My mother's dad got my mom a job in the lumber camps when she was 16. She was later cook in a boarding house in Fiborn Quarry, MI, a limestone quarry where my dad ran a general store and post office. Fiborn Quarry was near Rexton, where they got married and had their first three children—me and my two sisters. That's also where I started school.

When I was about eight, we moved to St. Ignace, where my dad went to work for the railroad. Later he worked on the railroad car ferry Chief Wawatam after the railroad business started to dwindle.

Our family wound up with 11 children. A boy died in infancy. I was the oldest, with three brothers and six sisters.

I believe my interest in boats started when I was a very young boy, when my Dad would make me toy boats to sail in a pond near our house. As I remember, the boats were really short boards, pointed at one end, with a couple of penciled sticks for spars. At that time there were many boats in that area—several fish tugs, the Michigan State car ferries, two large railroad car ferries (the Chief Wawatam and the Sainte Marie) plus passenger boats, Mackinac Island ferries and, occasionally, a commercial freighter with coal, cement and stone.

As a kid I used to hang around the passenger boat docks and occasionally carried baggage and other small tasks for spending money. I recall that I was fascinated with the passenger boat officers' uniforms, and hoped someday to be an officer myself, even a captain. As things came along, that's the only job I ever had after school: working on the boats. As soon as I finished high school, I got a job on the Michigan State car ferries to help the family.

In those days, quite a few passenger boats visited our town, among them the D & C side wheelers, the Eastern and Western States, the North and South America, the Alabama, Arnold's steam ferries to the island, and perhaps six to eight fishing tugs, along with the large steam tug Favorite with its barge Resolute.

I used to meet these boats and offer to carry the passenger bags for a dime or a quarter. I loved to watch the officers walk down the dock with their pressed uniforms and uniform caps.

One day a watchman started talking to me, and just before he turned to go back to his ship, he gave me his uniform cap with a gold cord across the front and a "watchman" band, and black satin top. I was in Seventh Heaven, really admired that cap—seldom took it off.

I was usually there to meet his boat and talk to him for a bit. One day, his boat came in and I waited and waited for him. He never showed. I was one disappointed kid.

While I was watching Arnold's steam ferry unload and load passengers for Mackinac Island, her captain, Hillard Bentzen, walked up to me and said, "Would you like to take a boat ride?" I was thrilled. To top that off, he asked me into the pilothouse and told the wheelsman to show me how to steer. Guess I wheeled for 10 minutes, and was delighted to steer that big boat. I hoped someday to become a sailor.

I recall my lower grade school years:
My first and second grades were in Fiborn Quarry, MI and my teacher was Hazel Small. I believe she was from the Cedarville area.
My third and fourth grades were spent at the Catholic school on top of the hill on Church Street in St. Ignace, and my teacher was a nun, a Rapin, named Sister Joseph. Her sister was my fifth and sixth grade teacher, Sister Ignatius, and she taught me the Spencerian method of penmanship. She used to award stars to the child with the best penmanship and to the one with the most improved penmanship, as well as a couple of other awards. I usually received the two golden stars for being the best and the most improved. Mother Gertrude taught 7th and 8th grades and was strict, but I liked her. (Then, too, we were getting older and larger; she had to be strict.)

Once three of us boys had to stay after school. The teacher had to leave the room for a bit, so went out and locked the door. One of my buddies liked to act like a cowboy. He had a lasso around his neck, tied one end to a desk and tossed the other end over the roof toward the ground. We drew straws to see who was to go out first. I lost, so had to go. My "cowboy" friend yelled, "Is the rope long enough?" and I told him, "It's just the right length." (But really, it was about 10 feet short). So the other two came down and had a surprise at the end of their trip.

One of the girl students who was always teased by the cowboy student saw him and reported us to the priest, who gave us a thrashing.

While attending high school I played sports (and didn't get the best grades in commercial law). I went along with two other students at night to crack a school window and get some of the semester exam questions.

About 10 p.m., armed with a flashlight, we climbed in the window and got the exam questions. One of the boys memorized the answers to 25 questions in commercial law. For some reason (suspicion?) the teacher reversed the order and had put Question #25 first. The only answer my friend got right was #13.

When I was growing up in the early 30s, right in the middle of the Depression, being the oldest of 10 children, I found things to be pretty tough. We always had a large truck garden, so were never lacking in vegetables. We had about two acres of apples, cherries and pear trees, so had ample fruit. We always had two milking cows and two horses to help with the farm work and with gathering wood for fuel. I can't remember when we didn't have venison, rabbit and fish in our house; seemed like we always did. We had a two-acre truck farm, so we always had our basement full of vegetables and apples. Dad always bought two young pigs and two heifers in the spring and butchered them through the winter. He'd hang them in the barn, with an axe and a saw nearby, because the meat would freeze as hard as ice.

We had an 80-acre farm on Cheeseman Road, so always had our own firewood. Two horses helped with the heavy work, and we also had two cows and a flock of 50 chickens. Although times were tough, we always had plenty to eat.

However, the "side goodies" were really scarce, things such as spending money and movies; and our clothes were few, and had to be kept in constant repair.

When I got into the early high school years and started checking out the girls, I never had change to buy them treats like the other guys had. So I figured the best way for me to make an impression was to excel at sports. Most of my leisure time was spent practicing, practicing and practicing, both football and basketball. I was lucky—being the biggest in my class, I had a slight edge on the other kids. But I'd still be out in the yard evenings, practicing until it got dark.

All that practicing paid off. I made the first team in both football and basketball in the ninth grade, and my last two years of high school I was "high point" most of the time in both sports.

I recall in my last year in school we were to play a "grudge" team, Rogers City. Mr. Saul Winkleman owned a drygoods store, and advertised for a month before the game that he'd give away a pair of shoes at that game to the one with the most points, the one with the most tackles, the one with the most blocks, and the one who caught the most passes.

We won.

And I got all four pairs of shoes.

On one of my running plays, Mr. Winkleman's son, Marvin, got in my way. I gave him a straight arm and he fell. He told me later that was the best block he had made all year; he took out two men.

We played Sault Ste. Marie, Ontario in high school football. I was fullback and did most of the punting. I recall that during one game we had a really strong headwind and I had to punt on our fourth down, so got off a good high punt, but the wind caught it and blew it back, and I caught my own punt. I don't remember the ruling on that, but we lost the game anyway.

We played Grand Marais in basketball on a Friday night, and after our games we usually had a school dance, and then stayed at the home of one of their players for the night. I danced most of the dances with a really pretty blonde, so she said, "Write to me, and I want the first dance when we go to St. Ignace." Some time later, Grand Marais came to St. Ignace to play, and after the game as I was going to the showers, this blonde cheerleader said, "Hurry up; I want the first dance."

As I was going down the stairs, the drummer banged on his drums and the Superintendent said, "All of you attending the dance will have to pay 25 cents—that includes the band, the players, every-one—to help sponsor the senior trip to Washington."

I tried borrowing nickels and dimes to make up a quarter, but couldn't. So I went out the side door, climbed a large maple tree in the middle of February, and watched my girl dancing with other guys. I was so horrified, I never wrote and told her my problem, and I never saw her again. But occasionally I still think of the incident.

I have a picture of our full 1934 basketball team coaches and players, two full rows, 18 of us. I was the tallest, so was holding the basketball. Of the 18 of us, only five are still living.

At Christmas time each of us 10 kids hung a sock. Our tree was ceiling high with lots of tinsel and popcorn strings all around, loads of icicles, wax candles clipped to the branches. The wood stove would get hot and the candles would look like wet noodles hanging down.

I remember my dad telling me that Christmas was coming on, seven kids and no money for gifts. His dad was a big man, a railroad guard. He got home about 7 a.m. on Christmas morning in a north-west gale, came running into the house all out of breath, saying, "Kids, kids, Santa's sleigh touched the fence when it was flying over it, and the toys spilled all over the field! Hurry and find them before they are covered with snow." He said they looked for toys all day.

During the 30s Dad had a Model A Ford that needed some work. So he took it to the Ford garage and said, "Fix it to the tune of $100; I've got 10 kids and that's all I can afford." So the garage man said, "Sign here to show you want the work done."

Some time later Dad checked on his car, and the work was done . . . with a bill for $200. The garage man told Dad the car needed the work, and he could stop in from time to time and pay what he could, $10 or so. At the end of a month, a sheriff's tow car was hooking onto Dad's car, which was parked in front of the house. I told Dad, and he got a 12-gauge shotgun and a 30-30 rifle, and walked out on the porch putting the shells into the guns. He told them, "If you make one more move towards that car, I'll shoot you. If you don't think I mean it—move!"

They jumped into their trucks and took off. A week later they were back and met the guns again, so they took off.

The lawyer called and said the garage was dishonest in what they had done, but that somehow it was still legal. So Dad told him, "Tell him he can tow it away in the morning."

That night, Dad said to us, "Don't go no place; we got a job to do." About 10 p.m. he said, "Let's go." We took all the wheels off and stood the car on blocks of wood. We took out the plugs, the seats, and threw the keys into the woods. What Dad had signed without reading was a 30-day mortgage.

The next morning the tow truck driver rapped on the door and said, "Where's the rest of your car?" Dad said, "She was all together when I went to bed." He had pushed it off the blocks before going to bed and it lay there like a pancake.

As a kid I used to help put up ice in Litchard's ice house. They wanted the ice in 24" cubes. The first field of ice we cut was 24" x 24" x 36" so we cut two more fields and waited until they were 24 x 24 x 24. We kept cutting on the same fields all winter. Today we have to wait until the middle of February to get four to six inches of ice in the Straits, in order for snowmobiles to cross safely to Mackinac Island.

When I was a kid, we all had sleighs, skis and skates. Now you seldom see a sleigh. A few of us would hitch our dogs to our sleighs. In extremely cold weather, we'd pile so much heavy woolen clothes on, we could hardly move. Now with heated 4-wheel drive trucks and nylon clothing, we're overly-warm all the time.

As a kid of about 15, I got angry with my dad and was going to run away from home. I had had it. So another kid and I jumped the railroad freight train and wound up in Marquette. We knew no one and were broke. We toughed it out for four days, eating mostly apples. Tiring of that menu we caught another freight for home, and figured afterwards that home was not so bad after all. I do remember that my dad never questioned me about my absence, and acted as if I'd never left.

Seemed I wasn't even missed.

I think growing up in a small town helped us kids. We always had a tree house out in the woods when we were young; as we got older, it was a hunting shack. We hunted mostly with sling shots or bows and arrows. In fact, I can't even remember having a gun around. Alongside our shack we always had a hole for our fire and barbecue pit, and a spit where we cooked our rabbits and fish. I recall that our outside cooking always tasted wonderful. . . no pepper or salt, no bread, but occasionally we'd have stew, if we could come up with the ingredients.

During the winter months we had a rabbit trap line, and set snares. We had a heavy screen where we'd cook our fish. I think my favorites were those perch. And the rabbits were pretty good, too.

We always had a set of stakes, where we'd play horse shoes. Some of us got pretty good.

We seldom roamed the streets like a lot of the other kids did. Occasionally we'd have a disagreement, and even a fight, but very seldom. Usually if the kids in my family didn't get along with one of us, they'd just sort of drift away for a while.

We seemed to be always building log rafts to fish from, and swimming took quite a bit of our summer time. Most of us had home

204

chores to do, also, so it wasn't all play. We had candles or a lantern for a night light, and an old radio or crystal set.

Occasionally girls would join us, usually the tomboy types who were as good as or better than we were with their slingshots or bows and arrows. We had one girl who could out-arm wrestle any of us boys, and could swim and run better than we could.

Usually we had some kind of pet—a crow, raccoon, or whatever came around. We'd feed them and they'd stay awhile.

Under the edge of our little wood pile we had a large box, which held our few tools and cookware, and the radio. Any time we left, all our gear went into the box, and a few sticks of wood were set over the top. We had benches made out of logs or poles, and never anything lying around. So nothing to steal, and no lock on our door. Our bed was the ground. Kids would join us for a while and then drift away, sometimes just coming back for a visit. We were all preteens to early teens. Two or three of us were altar boys in church, and Boy Scouts. I was both, and remember that at one time I wanted to be a priest, but just never made it.

I remember going ice fishing in the winter. We got three seven-foot poles, tied two of the ends together, and then formed a triangle with the third. We secured a tarp to two sides to form a lee. We'd place that to the wind-side for a shelter. With that, we could fish all day, throwing our catch on the ice. If biting was poor, we'd keep changing the position of our holes. Most of the time it was quite cold. I remember dumping the fish in the sink when we got home, and a half hour later our fish would thaw out and be flopping all over the kitchen.

We used to get up to four large perch on a line. Today we seldom ever see a perch, and it's been many years since I've seen a fish shanty on the ice.

Before going to bed at night, my mother put five gallons of

water near the kitchen stove, so we could have boiling water in the morning to pour over the towels wrapped around the water pipes in order to thaw them.

Today's kids live too fast a clip to ever be satisfied with our rural type of growing up. But I never smoked, and didn't know there was ever such a thing as "pot."

# *Animal Tales*

*I*was 2nd mate on the steamer *International.* We had a cook we called Val, who really liked the captain's little burgundy-colored cocker spaniel named Bozo. Bozo slept in the pilot house, and pretty much stayed forward, but would go back with the gang for meals.

In ports, Bozo (in his rope harness) and the cook always went up the street together. Our main ports were Chicago, Duluth, Superior and Escanaba, and there was always a tavern near by. When the bartender saw Val and Bozo coming, he's put out Bozo's large wooden bowl and the cook's large handled glass, both filled with draft beer. They'd drink and talk to each other until they had to return to the boat. Then both staggered back. As soon as they got on deck, the cook would take the guard harness off Bozo and he'd go forward to sleep in a shady spot.

One summer day, it was really sweltering hot. The deckhands swabbed the hallways with lye-water. (Today we can't use lye.) Then they rinsed the decks with clear water and put their half-full pails in the dunnage room instead of dumping them and rinsing out the pails, then stacking them.

Poor Bozo, really hot and panting, came into the dunnage room. Spying the buckets, he started drinking it, and of course it started burning his stomach. So he lay on deck. The watchman found me and asked what to do. I consulted the captain (it was his dog). I wanted to tie Bozo to a weight and toss him overboard, but the captain said, "Let's give him a few days." The dog lay there, not moving, for about three days with his tongue hanging out, eyes wide open. I was on watch, and looked out the back window and couldn't believe what I saw: Bozo, walking down the deck. He'd go about 30-35 feet, seemed to be on skates—his feet would spread out, and he'd slide down on his belly and just lie there. After about 15 seconds, he'd fight his way to his feet and start out again. He kept repeating this routine until finally he got to the screened galley door. He sat down and barked once. The cook came out crying, and said, "Bozo, you came back to see me."

Bozo laid his face across the cook's highs and died. There wasn't a dry eye on the boat.

We got a large piece of canvas, laid a couple of heavy grate bars on it, laid Bozo on the bars, wrapped the canvas tight and sewed him up. We laid him on a long wooden plank. The 2nd cook said a prayer, and we slowly raised the plank and he slid into the water. We had a pretty quiet boat that night; it was like losing one of us.

When our boys were around 10 or 12 years old, my wife's brother gave them a tiny German shepherd puppy. We had to feed him with a small baby bottle. The kids called him Bruno, and he turned out to be a beautiful dog. One ear was pencil straight and the other flopped over a little on the end.

Bruno was really possessive of the boys until they got older, then he took care of my sister's kids next door, and finally our grand daughters. My nephew shot a deer and hung it from an apple tree in front of their house, and that dog, on his own, lay under the tree and guarded that deer.

The little girls would be swinging and the dog lying down and watching them. If the kids started swinging too high, the dog would bark and raise hell. The girls would take the dog to the State Park, where they had swings and slides. One slide had a nine-foot ladder that went almost straight up to a slide with a hump in the middle. The kids would stand in line and take their turn to climb up and slide down. The dog would be in line, waiting his turn, also. A German shepherd normally is not a water dog. My wife's mother was an excellent swimmer; she'd go out about 50 feet and swim parallel to the shore; the dog would swim with her.

Another time my little nephew cut down a small Christmas tree in the State Park. Someone called the local police, so they came up to discipline the boy, but they couldn't put him in the squad car unless the dog went in, also. They got him to the station and couldn't do anything with the dog there. So they called my wife to come down and get the boy and dog. The dog hated cats, but somewhere along the way, he took up with a tiny kitten, and no dog could come near that kitten. They slept together in Bruno's doghouse. The cat got to be eight or nine months old and took off one day. We saw it once or twice after that.

When Bruno got to be near 15 years old, his hind quarters started to fail and he was going blind. We had to put him to sleep. No dry eyes for quite a time. Everyone missed Bruno.

I had a watchman on the City of Milwaukee, a Lake Michigan car ferry. He was a farmer with four children, and always liked pets. One day his pig had a litter of six, and among them was a very small one that was colorful, like a calico cat, three or four different colors. The kids adopted him for their pet. He followed them all over, even in the house most of the time. The family had a station wagon and used to take the pig along on family picnics. In the meantime, the pig kept growing until it was about 500 pounds, and still the kids continued to play with it. One Sunday, while going on a picnic, they left the pig and locked the screen door of their house (but not the regular door). The pig crashed the screen door, rooted up the wall-to-wall carpeting, and tore up one end of the sofa. It was their pet, so they felt they couldn't butcher him, but they sold him. My watchman said his kids cried for a few days.

He also raised a pet crow, and said that crow would bring everything home, especially anything shiny.

I knew a waitress, a farm girl living in Moran, MI. She had two small pigs for pets. Pigs are the smartest animals on a farm. They followed her like puppies and never, ever messed in the house. They would "sit" and "stay" when she told them and never left the yard.

Coming down the St. Mary's River, when approaching Barbeau, I always blew a salute—one long and two short toots on the ship's whistle—when abreast the Swartz's home. They had a little white terrier who'd always run to the fence, barking at us. I saluted that dog for about five years. I got so attached to it, I even sent it a couple of rawhide bones at Christmas one year. Then one trip down, the dog didn't show. Later I got a letter saying that the dog had died; he had lived 14 years.

Going through the Keweenaw waterway through Houghton, we often saw eagles and occasionally saw one scoop up a fish.

Wheeling on the A. B. Wolvin, I once saw a moose swimming across the St. Mary's River. We slowed down to give it more time. That was in 1939, and was the only time I ever saw a moose. We often saw deer along the banks of the river.

Coming into DeTour fuel dock we saw two adult foxes with three pups. The foreman told us he had often seen that fox family.

Coming back to the boat one day in Duluth, eating a chocolate bar, I met a little burgundy-colored cocker spaniel about four months old. I gave it a piece of candy and then rationed the bar until I got to the boat. I gave her the last piece, tucked her under my arm and climbed the ladder. She turned out to be a lady dog, and after about a month she developed a bad habit of barking at night.

As I was taking her for a walk in Buffalo, a little boy fell in step with me. He was about 12 years old, and really took to the dog we had named Lady. So I gave him the pup, and he was truly pleased. The following year, he came down to the boat with a little red male puppy for me, wrapped in an old sweater. I really didn't want the dog, but didn't want to disappoint him, either. I called the wife to meet me in

Duluth, and she took the dog, which we named Rusty, a wavy-haired short-tailed pup.

We had that dog for about 15 years, a really beautiful dog. He finally went blind and I had to put him to sleep. My wife and I and the two boys all cried over the loss of Rusty.

We had a cocker spaniel on board once, a friendly dog except with one watchman. One noon, while we were coming into Duluth and still about three miles out, the watchman kicked the dog over the side. I told the mate to pay him off right now and call for another watchman.

About 7 p.m., while we were loading grain, the little dog came barking at the foot of the ladder. The whole crew was pleased to see that little guy.

I was captain on the William A. Reiss one spring when we were leaving the Locks and the lockmaster called to inform me that there was a family of beavers on a slab of ice floating down toward us. We rang full speed to get steerage, and then shut the engine off. We were able to scoot around the beavers and the lockmaster then locked the animals through by themselves.

Another time, while leaving DeTour southbound in the spring, I noticed a field of ice with about eight deer on it. I called the Coast Guard and they said they'd take care of the deer. I never heard if they did or not.

Before we had radar, in the early 40s, we had Cindy, a black cocker spaniel aboard. In really thick, dense fog, when approaching rivers or harbors where they had an approach bell buoy, we always had two or three crew look-outs on the bow, watching and listening for the bell buoy, along with Cindy.

We were right in front of the pilot house, near the steering pole. On either side of the stem were mooring chalks, about 10 inches in diameter, through which we passed cables. All of a sudden Cindy would put her nose down to one of the openings and growl. We'd go to that side of the stem, and sure enough, the buoy would soon pop up. She never missed.

Cindy always did her "job" between #3 and #4 hatches, in the same spot. We had a water hose hooked up there, and the watchman would rinse the deck before breakfast. She picked that spot herself.

She always slept under the captain's chair in the pilot house. If she passed a little gas, they'd yell at her. She'd squat down and hug the deck. But if she wasn't guilty, she'd flare up and growl.

She spent the winters on the boat with the "ship keeper"; the marine insurance company insisted on a caretaker during winter months. Cindy spent her whole life on the boat. Her 14th year, they took her off the boat and she died shortly afterwards.

My wife, Lou, had an uncle who was a surveyor and lived in a cabin in the woods with his dog Susie. One night he had fish for supper, wrapped the scraps in a newspaper, but forgot to toss the bundle in the outside garbage barrel. Come nightfall, he called for Susie to come in for the night, but this night she stayed under the cabin. Sometime later a bear, smelling the fish, came and knocked the barrel over. Not finding the fish scraps, he slammed the cabin. Little Susie was quick and began nipping at the bear's "heels." The bear got so nervous he took off.

Years later the uncle came visiting with the little dog, who was now blind and feeble. I told him, "You're not doing that dog a favor by keeping her around. Why don't you give her a one-way ride?" He answered, "Susie saved my life from that bear; I'll care for her as long as she's around.

My dad had a beautiful black mare and was always bragging how great this horse was. So one day a couple of guys bet him that the horse couldn't pull a boxcar past a railroad crossing, about 50 feet. Dad said, "You're on," and hitched the horse to the trunk of the boxcar. The horse got right down and started pulling. Finally the car started moving and she pulled it through the crossing—but in so doing she went blind from the strain. A cataract film had formed over the horse's eyes, and about once a month Dad would crease a piece of paper, put a purplish talcum powder in the crease, and then blow the powder into the horse's eye. The powder would cut the film and she'd be able to see for a while.

One winter a fellow from Mackinac Island came over to buy the horse. Later the buyer said to my dad, "You lied to me. You said this was a good horse; she's blind." Dad said, "Oh, no, I didn't lie. I told you she didn't look too good, but she's a damned good horse."

Cats were always considered bad luck, and seldom if ever were they allowed on board, although dogs were.

A watchman quit once, and while getting off he was carrying a cloth-covered bird cage, so I asked one of the guys, "What does he have, a parrot?" "No," he said, "that's his pet white rat." He'd have been gone a lot sooner had I known that.

The only time I was ever fired, the captain's spoiled son got a job on the boat. He was a mean kid; he'd shoot seagulls with a B-B gun, and abuse kids younger and smaller than he was. The 2nd mate had a nice little beagle with very long ears. One day as I was coming down the deck I saw the kid pick up the little dog by the ears. The dog thrashed his legs and squealed, trying to get free. I told the captain's son to drop the dog and he told me to get lost. So I swung a hay maker at him, catching him on the chin. He fell to the deck, knocked out cold. The captain fired me, but I was not sorry. I would have done it again.

I was 2nd mate on the International, and our runs were mostly Marquette to South Chicago's steel mills. It took us about 2½ days each way, five days for a round trip. Our watchman caught an injured pigeon on deck; it could use only one leg. So he put a light splint on the injured leg and kept it locked up for about three weeks or so. Then, since it was getting along pretty well, he removed the splint and let it go on deck. The bird flew around, and at night came back to its box. We'd get to port and the bird would take off.

Later, when leaving port, the captain would blow three blasts on the deep-throated whistle and the pigeon would come flying back. This happened at both ends of our route for about six weeks. Then one day the bird didn't show. We kept watching for it. Some of the crew would claim they saw it, but I doubt that they did. We missed our bird buddy.

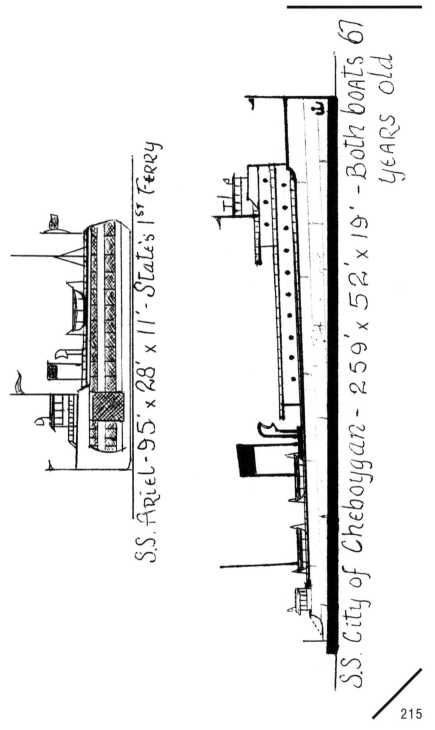

S.S. Ariel - 95' x 28' x 11' - State's 1st Ferry

S.S. City of Cheboygan - 259' x 52' x 19' - Both boats 67 years old

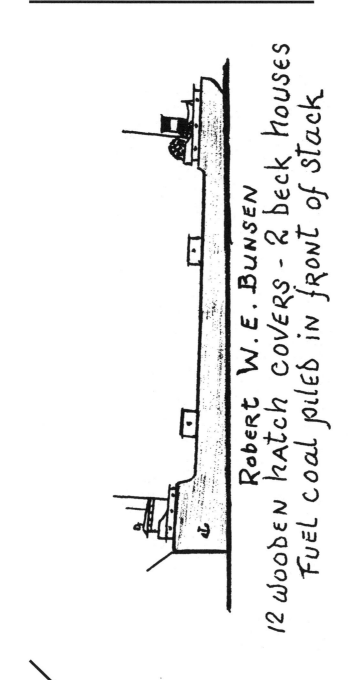

Robert W.E. Bunsen
12 wooden hatch covers - 2 beck houses
fuel coal piled in front of stack

In the early 1800's, boats & barges averaged 150' long. & the steam-boat often towed up to 5 barges; the barges often carried more cargo than the steam boat.. & recall steam boats & 2 barges, averaging 450 ft. long...

*Miscellaneous ships from the pen of Ray I. McGrath:*

*Miscellaneous ships from the pen of Ray I. McGrath:*

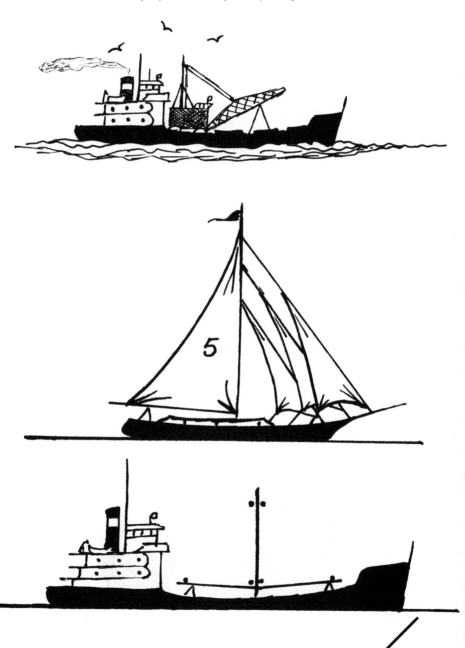

*Miscellaneous ships from the pen of Ray I. McGrath:*

# V

*Glossary*

*&*

*Index*

*Hope the mates stay awake and the weather stays clear—*

# Glossary

| | |
|---|---|
| **AB** | Able-bodied seaman |
| **A-B** | A seaman can perform all duties aboard, and passes a Coast Guard test to prove it. |
| **Abaft** | Anything toward the stern (back end) of a vessel |
| **Abandon ship** | Immediately leave ship because of an emergency |
| **Abeam** | Abreast the boatside, at right angles to it |
| **Aboard** | Upon or in the boat |
| **Above board** | Open and visible; also meaning open and fair dealings |
| **Abreast** | Anything at right angles to the ship—a lighthouse, boat, etc. |
| **Adrift** | Anything floating at random |
| **Advance** | Usually meaning to get part of one's pay before pay-day |
| **Advice boat** | Small boat used to carry orders to passing ships (no longer used since radios are aboard) |
| **Afloat** | Vessel wholly supported by water, clear of ground |
| **Aft** | At, near or toward the stern |
| **After-body** | Anything on board that's aft of amidship |
| **Aground** | When a vessel is resting on ground, or is stranded |
| **Ahead** | Opposite of stern; any distance directly ahead of ship |
| **Ahoy** | Normal "hail" to a ship to attract attention |
| **Aids to navigation** | buoys, lights, fog signals, or any other charted charted information to help for safe navigation |
| **All hands** | All persons on board, report to main deck—usually because of an emergency, and all help is needed |
| **All standing** | Usually meaning to stop ship's way suddenly by use of her anchor |
| **Alley way** | Usually meaning a small passage way to cabins or other parts of the vessel |
| **Almanac** | (Nautical)—publication containing positions of celestial bodies for use in plotting |
| **Aloft** | Overhead—masts, rigging, or anything high |
| **Alow** | Opposite of "aloft"—on or near the ship's deck |
| **Amain** | Old maritime saying meaning, "Let go anchor at |

once;" today's sailors wouldn't know the meaning of the word.

**Amidships**  Anything near the midsection of a ship

**Anchor**  A huge, heavy instrument designed to hold the ship and prevent her from drifting; usually positioned on either side of the stem and usually six to eight feet above the water line. An anchor can be dropped within a few seconds.

**Anchor light**  Two white lights on the fore and after spar, 20–40 feet above deck; can be seen from any angle of approach to inform other vessels you are anchored. This is also accompanied by the continuous ringing of ship's bell, upon the approach of another vessel

**Anchorage**  Good holding area to anchor; shown on ships' charts

**Athwartships**  Crosswise to or in the boat

**A-trip**  An anchor is said to be A-trip when it is broken out of the ground, or when it's holding position, usually by the pull of the windlass (a steam engine used to hoist the anchor)

**Autopilot**  A mechanical device used to steer the boat automatically

**Avast**  A term used to stop operation, or to hold or stand by

**Awash**  Where an object is almost submerged, as when seas wash over a wreck or a rock

**Aweigh**  Same meaning as "Atrip," when anchor is broken out of its holding position and the ship is liable to drift. The more anchor chain you use when anchoring, the more securely the anchor will hold. Often two anchors are used to lessen the boat's swing.

**Baboon watch**  Denotes a man selected to stand, usually ladder watch, to be sure no undesirables come aboard. Usually the apprentices were selected while the others went ashore. This term is not used today.

**Ballast**  Water purposely put in the boat to make it more seaworthy and to ride more comfortably.

**Ballast tanks**  The water described above is stowed in ballast tanks so the water won't go astray and cause the ship to list.

These tanks are located just above the keel.

**Bald-headed** Sailing vessel underway without her headsails set

**Barge** Years ago a barge was built like a steamboat except that it had no engine. It had to depend on another boat for propulsion. Normally the barge's cargo was often as much as or more than that of the steamboat. Often a steamboat could tow two of these barges in tandem, one following the other.

**Batten down** In older vessels, hatches were closed and then a canvas tarp was secured over the hatch to prevent water seepage. Then channel irons were placed on top of the tarps, usually six placed fore and aft to the ship's heading. Then perhaps two channel irons, crosswise to the hatch, would hold the other channels down. Today's boats are much higher and have a different hatch system, so tarps are no longer used.

**Beachcomber** A sea man who preferred to hang around ports and harbors, existing on the charity of others. We still have a few of this type of deadbeats.

**Beam** The width of a vessel at her widest point

**Bearing** Usually an angle taken on a shore light, to figure a ship's distance off a light or vessel's speed. A bearing taken on a light at 45° and time taken, then again when light is exactly abeam, abreast or 90° from bow. The time between the two bearings is the distance in time you are off the shore light.

**Becket** Normally an eye is spliced on the end of a mooring wire to toss over a dock spile in order to secure the vessel. On the end of this 8- to 10-foot cable eye, a small cable is spliced to form a half-circle hand-hold

**Beetle** Heavy mallet used by shipwrights (shipyard workers)

**Bell** A heavy ship's bell placed on top of her pilot house for denoting the time or for sounding in the fog. Bell is made of heavy brass, about 10–to–18 inches, with the vessel's name engraved on it. When a ship is scrapped, her bell usually commands a high sale price. I've got one that strikes quarter hours, half hours and hours. A six-inch ship's brass clock goes for about $700.

**Bell rope**   A short length of rope hanging over the wheelsman's head, that he uses to denote the ship's time by the working four-hour watches, from one bell to eight bells. The half hours are one bell and the hours are two bells (so 12:30, 4:30 and 8:30 are 1 bell; 1, 5 and 9 o'clock are 2 bells; 1:30, 5:30 and 9:30 are 2 bells and then 1 bell—ding-ding, followed by ding); 7:30 would be ding-ding, ding-ding, ding-ding, and then 1 more ding; 4, 8 and 12 o'clock would be ding-ding, ding-ding, ding-ding, ding-ding.

**Belly**   Broadest part of a boat's hull, below the water line

**Below**   Underneath the boat's deck; lower living quarters

**Berth**   A place to sleep—your narrow bunk or bed; dockside storage for the boat; or a term used to indicate clearance of danger, or to give a wide berth to a shoal point of land or a rock.

**Bight**   A piece of rope in the shape of a U; the same applies to a piece of land that is shaped like a U, or a harbor.

**Bilge**   The lowest part of a boat, normally used for ballast water

**Bill of Health**   A certificate signifying all crew members have passed the health inspection

**Bill of Lading**   The master gets a receipt of all goods and their condition, and promises to deliver goods in the same condition they were when he received them.

**Binnacle**   A wooden cylinder like a column, about five feet high, housing the ship's compass and its steel ball correctors. The balls are about five inches in diameter, and are on either side of the 10-inch magnetic cord. Binnacle usually has a clear glass dome over it and a rheostat light.

**Bird's nest**   (Crow's nest) on the forward spar, usually about 40 feet above the deck, where a lookout may be placed to spot other ships or shore lights in fog. Lookouts were equipped with speaking-tube and compass, so

| | |
|---|---|
| | you had contact with the pilot house. |
| **Bite** | When a dropped anchor suddenly holds firm without dragging |
| **Bitter end** | When all the ship's anchor cable has been run out |
| **Blister** | Small patch of delamination in a fiberglass hull |
| **Boa** | The front portion of a boat |
| **Boatswain's chair** | A short board secured in a bridle and used for painting the spars or swinging a man over onto a dock when tying up. |
| **Bollard** | A vertical piece of iron or timber fixed to the ground for securing a ship's mooring wires when docking. |
| **Bone** | The white foam under a ship's stem; when she's underway she's said to have a bone in her teeth. |
| **Boom** | A deckhand's boom is about 16 feet long, with a snatch block at the end and a welded cleat at the heel, to run the deckhand's chair-line through. That way you can control his decline to the dock. This boom is usually a four-inch heavy-duty steam pipe. |
| **Bowline** | A knot tied in such a way as to produce an eye or loop in the end of a rope. This has many uses at sea, and cannot slip or jam. |
| **Bracket** | A triangular bracket to support anything beyond hull |
| **Breakwall** | An artificially-placed construction in or around a harbor, designed to break the force of the sea and to provide shelter for vessels lying within main cable and the dock spiling. |
| **Breeches Buoy** | A ring lifebuoy fitted with canvas breeches and used for life saving when a ship has run aground or is in danger of breaking up. Contact with the ship is made from ashore by means of a line fired from a rocket gun. A line is then rigged up from ship to shore, and the breech buoy with person is hauled to shore and back again until all the crew is off the boat. |
| **Bulkhead** | The upright partition separating one compartment from another |
| **Cable** | Often referred to as the anchor chain |
| **Camouflage** | Method of disguising the size outline, course and |

speed of a ship by painting her hull and upper works in contrasting shapes and colors.

**Canbuoy** Buoy in the form of a truncated cone, normally painted red or red and white, indicating the port side of a channel, and numbered in even numbers

**Capsize** To upset or overturn; used in connection with a vessel at sea or in a harbor. Generally this term is used in relation to natural causes, such as high winds or seas, but also refers to human error, such as faulty cargo stowage.

**Catamaran** Any boat built with two hulls, side by side, making riding more comfortable

**Come home** An anchor is said to "come home" when its flukes are not holding and it drags.

**Course** Direction of travel, usually given in degrees

**Davit** A small cast-iron crane fitted with hoisting and lowering gear, in the form of blocks and tackle. It is used with older radial davits to swing out and lower lifeboats.

**Davy Jones' Locker** On ship it's the equivalent to the graveyard for sailors; "deep six" means the same thing, anything thrown over the side.

**Dead ahead** Immediately in front of the boat, or in its apparent direction

**Dead reckoning** A position which is obtained by applying courses and distances made through the water from the last-known observed position

**Dead work** An old term meaning all the ship that is above water. Today we call it free board.

**Derelict** A vessel abandoned at sea. When a ship is abandoned, whether by consent, compulsion or stress of weather, she is a derelict and free to whoever finds her. However, if there is a living cat or dog aboard, the owner may recover the ship within a year, by paying the salvage, if he so wishes.

**Detente** A notch in the shifting lever of the engine control

**Deviation** Magnetic compass error caused by boats' magnetism,

228

or by some iron object distracting the compass, such as a bridge

**Diaphone** A type of sound signal emitted from lighthouses and light vessels in the fog. It is characterized by a powerful, low note, ending with a sharply descending tone known as the grunt.

**Displacement** The weight of a boat; also the weight of fluid displaced when floating

**Double bottom** The space between the outer skin on the bottom of a ship and the water-tight plating over the floor. A double bottom serves two purposes: first, as a protection against disaster when the bottom is pierced; and second, as a convenient stowage for liquid ballast.

**Draft** The maximum distance a hull extends under the surface of the water; also called the load line, indicated by painted numbers at each end

**Dunnage** Loose wood or wooden blocks, used in the cargo holds to secure cargo; also sometimes referred to as a small room for odd things, such as assorted tools

**Ensign** A flag flown by a ship to denote its nationality

**EPIRB** Emergency Position Indicating Radio Beacon—a safety device sending a signal to indicate a ship's position

**Even keel** A ship is said to be on even keel when she's floating exactly upright.

**Fantail** The overhanging part of a ship's stern, often used to stow a tow line and rope. Also refers to the area where the steering gear winch or machine is often placed.

**Fathometer** A sounder indicating water's depth

**Fender** An appliance used to let something down along the dock-side of a ship, to ward off a heavy bump when the ship strikes the dock. Is also a term used to ward off a small boat in making a dock, usually with an oar or boat hook.

**Figure eight** A knot formed like an "8" and used to prevent the loose end of a rope, from passing through a block

| | |
|---|---|
| **Fix** | A calculated position obtained by use of a sextant or by other means |
| **Flotsam** | Usually referred to as wreckage from a ship, floating on the water, like ship's furniture, buoys, etc. |
| **Fluke** | The two flat blades of an anchor that dig into the ground, giving the anchor holding power |
| **Fog signals** | A series of sound signals on a ship's main whistle, to warn others in a fog—usually one prolonged blast every two seconds. Today, with radar, fog signals are not much used. |
| **Forecastle** | Pronounced "foc'sle"—the area on a boat directly in front of the pilothouse to the stem; also referred to as the living area for the crew on the deck. |
| **Forward** | Toward the front of a vessel |
| **Frame** | Any one of the many ribs of a ship; it's structure |
| **Free board** | The distance from the main deck to the water line |
| **GPS** | Global Positioning System—a system of navigation using satellites and a receiver aboard, to determine a ship's position; this method is nearly exact. |
| **Gain** | Quality found in various electronic instruments and equipment related to the strength of the signal |
| **Gale** | A storm in which the wind is blowing from 34 to 47 knots |
| **Galley** | The name usually used for the ship's kitchen |
| **Grapple hook** | A bar that is usually about five feet long, to which three prongs formed in a half circle are welded at one end with sharp outside ends, and a ring is on the top end with a rope fastened to it. This grapple hook can be thrown into the water to try to recover an object, such as a metal ladder. |
| **Gunwale** | The upper edge of a ship's side or hull |
| **Gyrocompass** | Compass employing a gyroscope to give it direction; far more true than magnetic compasses |
| **Half hitch** | A single rope around a spar; one of many sailor knots |
| **Hatch** | An opening in the deck, equipped with hatch cover, usually hinged and water-tight |
| **Hawse pipe** | Part of a ship's bow, where the anchor-windlass |

(winch) is located. A large pipe runs down to either side of the bow, used for the heavy chain secured to the anchor. Also a term used to a person's trip "up the ladder" to become captain. Saying, "He came up the hawse pipe" means he worked his way up in every position from deck hand to captain. Today many captains start out in a maritime school, and come out with a mate's license, never having been on a ship. Then he secures a job as 3rd mate, then 2nd, then 1st, and finally captain. I would far rather be with the Hawse pipe captain.

**Head** On a boat it's the equivalent to the bathroom in your home.

**Helm** Device by which a boat is steered

**Hog** Refers to a ship supported by a huge wave at its center, and hardly any water at each end—"a hogging stress." Opposite true when the ship is supported by two huge waves at either end and no supporting water in the middle—referred to as "sagging."

**Hook** Slang for anchor; "on the hook" means anchored.

**Horsepower** Power of the engine; today's larger boats have from 8,000 to 20,000 horsepower.

**Hull** The outside covering or skin of a ship below the deck line; also term to denote an abandoned ship at sea

**Inboard** Anywhere on the boat

**Jettison** This is the act of throwing goods or equipment over the side to lighten the ship in stress of weather or other danger.

**Kapok** A silky fiber found in pods of trees in West Africa, used for life preservers

**Keel** The center line protruding from ship's hull to bottom; part of the ship's construction

**Ketch** A two-masted sailing vessel

**Kill switch** A main switch on engine or pilot house control panel that will shut down everything, in case of an emergency

**Knot** In your car it would be miles per hour; on boats it's

|  |  |
|---|---|
|  | knots. Miles are 5,280 feet; knots are 6,080 feet. |
| **Lifeline** | A cable normally about one-eighth of an inch thick, strung from forward to aft on a ship, and its sag point in the middle. It may be strung about eight feet above deck. On either end of this line a canvas is secured, in which about 10-foot lines are stored. The other ends of the three-quarter-inch rope lines are spliced into three-inch steel rings, which are threaded through the lifeline leading onto the deck. In extreme weather these guide lines or lifelines are used to prevent crew from being washed over the side in heavy weather. I've been in many storms with these lines available, but never used one. It never was that important to risk my life just to go aft. |
| **Listing** | Leaning one way or the other |
| **Loran** | Navigational system that positions your vessel by means of shore-based stations and a ship's receiver |
| **Loudhailer** | A device used to magnify your voice |
| **Mast** | A pole-like structure usually from 20-40 feet high, equipped with navigational lights, anchor lites and antennas, and supported with guy wires |
| **May Day** | A distress signal used in extreme emergencies |
| **Mooring** | To secure a boat to a shore-based land structure like a dock |
| **Nautical mile** | This measures 6,088 feet; a standard mile is 5,280 feet. |
| **Pelorus** | Compass card, fitted with sight vanes and used to take bearings on distant objects |
| **Pile or Pilings** | A heavy post driven into the ground or lake, or secured to docks to secure vessels |
| **Port** | Usually a harbor or shelter where boats can dock or anchor; also a term for lefthand side of boat |
| **Power plant** | The engine room of a boat |
| **Radar** | An electronic device used in navigation to pinpoint location |
| **Range** | A set of high markers, usually in shallow areas, to indicate the deep channel; the far marker is usually taller and both sets have lights. When these lights are |

|  | lined up, you're in the center of the channel. The ranges are about ¼ miles apart. |
| **Rudder** | A vertical rectangular structure aft of a boat's propeller, used to steer by |
| **Running attitude** | The angle a boat interfaces with the water while it is underway |
| **Running gear** | Could mean any tools or added structure used while underway; could even mean rain gear, winter gear, clothes, etc. |
| **Sea way** | Motion of the waves |
| **Sextant** | Device to measure angles of celestial bodies, used in navigation to seek your position |
| **Slip** | Any channel between a couple of docks, where boats are kept or worked on |
| **Sounding** | Shows water depth and shoals, and type of water bottom—sand, gravel etc. |
| **Stability** | Boat's ability to return to original position after listing |
| **Starboard** | Righthand side of boat |
| **Stock** | The heavy central part of an anchor to which the chain is attached |
| **Tender** | A small service boat or errand boat |
| **Transom** | The surface of a boat at the extreme stern |
| **Twin-screw** | Two propellers drive and greatly assist in handling boat |
| **Variation** | Compass error caused by earth's magnetic and geographical earth poles |
| **Wake** | The water track left behind a traveling boat |
| **Waypoint** | A theoretical or actual point used in navigation as a goal or an intermediate goal |
| **Wheel** | A screw propeller |
| **Wheelhouse** | Pilothouse cabin from which the boat is navigated |
| **Windlass** | A hoisting machine, often called anchor windlass, to hoist the anchor |

*Today's boats are so huge, many of the terms in this Glossary no longer apply. In my day the largest boat was 600 feet long. Today the largest is 1,013.5 feet long.*

# Index